CUSTOM CURRICULUM

"They're Not Like Us!"

Fran and Jill Sciacca

Randy Petersen

David C. Cook Publishing Co.
Elgin, Illinois—Paris, Ontario

Custom Curriculum
"They're Not Like Us!"

© 1994 David C. Cook Publishing Co.

All rights reserved. Except for the reproducible student sheets, which may be copied for ministry use, no part of this book may be reproduced in any form without the written permission of the publisher, unless otherwise noted in the text.

Unless otherwise noted, Scripture quotations are from the Holy Bible, New International Version (NIV), © 1973, 1978, 1984 by International Bible Society. Used by permission of Zondervan Bible Publishers.

Published by David C. Cook Publishing Co.
850 North Grove Ave., Elgin, IL 60120
Cable address: DCCOOK
Series creator: John Duckworth
Series editor: Randy Southern
Editor: Randy Southern
Option writers: Stan Campbell, Sue Reck, Randy Southern, and Mark Syswerda
Designer: Bill Paetzold
Cover illustrator: Glen Hanson
Inside illustrator: Jackie Besteman
Printed in U.S.A.

ISBN: 0-7814-5146-9

CONTENTS

About the Authors — 4

You've Made the Right Choice! — 5

Opportunity, Not Difficulty!
by Fran and Jill Sciacca — 9

Publicity Clip Art — 14

Sessions by Randy Petersen
Options by Stan Campbell, Sue Reck, Randy Southern, and Mark Syswerda

Session One
So Many Flavors
(Why Different Churches Believe Different Things) — 16

Session Two
The Big Three
(An Overview of Protestant, Catholic, and Orthodox Beliefs) — 32

Session Three
Who's Protesting What?
(An Overview of the Major Protestant Denominations) — 48

Session Four
When the Spirit Moves
(What Pentecostals and Charismatics Believe) — 64

Session Five
Common Ground and Negotiables
(Affirming the Common Heritage of the Church Universal) — 80

About the Authors

Randy Petersen is a free-lance writer living in Westville, New Jersey. Formerly the executive editor of *Evangelical Newsletter* and *The Bible Newsletter*, he has also worked with young people and written several books for the youth market, including *O.T. Speedway* and *N.T. Speedway* in the Custom Curriculum series.

Stan Campbell has been a youth worker for almost twenty years and has written several books on youth ministry including the BibleLog series (SonPower) and the Quick Studies series (David C. Cook). Among the books he's written in the Custom Curriculum series are *Hormone Helper, Just Look at You! What Would Jesus Do?* and *Your Bible's Alive!* Stan and his wife, Pam, are youth directors at Lisle Bible Church in Lisle, Illinois.

Sue Reck is an editor for Chariot Family Products. She is also a free-lance curriculum writer. She has worked with young people in Sunday school classes, youth groups, and camp settings.

Randy Southern is a product developer of youth material at David C. Cook and the series editor of Custom Curriculum. He has also worked on such products as Quick Studies, Incredible Meeting Makers, Snap Sessions, First Aid for Youth Groups, Junior Highs Only, and Pathfinder Electives.

Mark Syswerda is an associate editor of youth products at David C. Cook. In addition to working with youth groups, he has contributed to such youth resources as the *Quick Studies B.C.* and *Great Groups* series (David C. Cook).

You've Made the Right Choice!

Thanks for choosing **Custom Curriculum!** We think your choice says at least three things about you:

(1) You know your group pretty well, and want your program to fit that group like a glove;

(2) You like having options instead of being boxed in by some far-off curriculum editor;

(3) You have a small mole on your left forearm, exactly two inches below the elbow.

OK, so we were wrong about the mole. But if you like having choices that help you tailor meetings to fit your kids, **Custom Curriculum** *is* the best place to be.

Going through Customs

In this (and every) **Custom Curriculum** volume, you'll find
- five great sessions you can use anytime, in any order.
- reproducible student handouts, at least one per session.
- a truckload of options for adapting the sessions to your group (more about that in a minute).
- a helpful get-you-ready article by a youth expert.
- clip art for making posters, fliers, and other kinds of publicity to get kids to your meetings.

Each **Custom Curriculum** session has three to six steps. No matter how many steps a session has, it's designed to achieve these goals:

- *Getting together.* Using an icebreaker activity, you'll help kids to be glad they came to the meeting.
- *Getting thirsty.* Why should kids care about your topic? Why should they care what the Bible has to say about it? You'll want to take a few minutes to earn their interest before you start pouring the "living water."
- *Getting the Word.* By exploring and discussing carefully selected passages, you'll find out what God has to say.
- *Getting the point.* Here's where you'll help kids make the leap from principles to nitty-gritty situations they are likely to face.
- *Getting personal.* What should each group member do as a result of this session? You'll help each person find a specific "next step" response that works for him or her.

Each session is written to last 45 to 60 minutes. But what if you have less time—or more? No problem! **Custom Curriculum** is all about . . . options!

What Are My Options?

Every **Custom Curriculum** session gives you fourteen kinds of options:

• *Extra Action*—for groups that learn better when they're physically moving (instead of just reading, writing, and discussing).
• *Combined Junior High/High School*—to use when you're mixing age levels, and an activity or case study would be too "young" or "old" for part of the group.
• *Small Group*—for adapting activities that would be tough with groups of fewer than eight kids.
• *Large Group*—to alter steps for groups of more than twenty kids.
• *Urban*—for fitting sessions to urban facilities and multiethnic (especially African-American) concerns.
• *Heard It All Before*—for fresh approaches that get past the defenses of kids who are jaded by years in church.
• *Little Bible Background*—to use when most of your kids are strangers to the Bible, or haven't made a Christian commitment.
• *Mostly Guys*—to focus on guys' interests and to substitute activities they might be more enthused about.
• *Mostly Girls*—to address girls' concerns and to substitute activities they might prefer.
• *Extra Fun*—for longer, more "rowdy" youth meetings where the emphasis is on fun.
• *Short Meeting Time*—tips for condensing the session to 30 minutes or so.
• *Fellowship & Worship*—for building deeper relationships or enabling kids to praise God together.
• *Media*—to spice up meetings with video, music, or other popular media.
• *Sixth Grade*—appearing only in junior high/middle school volumes, this option helps you change steps that sixth graders might find hard to understand or relate to.
• *Extra Challenge*—appearing only in high school volumes, this option lets you crank up the voltage for kids who are ready for more Scripture or more demanding personal application.

Each kind of option is offered at least twice in each session. So in this book, you get *almost 150* ways to tweak the meetings to fit your group!

Customizing a Session

All right, you may be thinking. *With all of these options flying around, how do I put a session together? I don't have a lot of time, you know.*

We know! That's why we've made **Custom Curriculum** as easy to follow as possible. Let's take a look at how you might prepare an actual meeting. You can do that in four easy steps:

(1) *Read the basic session plan.* Start by choosing one or more of the goals listed at the beginning of the session. You have three to pick from: a goal that emphasizes *knowledge,* one that stresses *understanding,* and one that emphasizes *action.* Choose one or more, depending on what *you* want to accomplish. Then read the basic plan to see what will work for you and what might not.

(2) *Choose your options.* You don't *have* to use any options at all; the

basic session plan would work well for many groups, and you may want to stick with it if you have absolutely no time to consider options. But if you want a more perfect fit, check out your choices.

As you read the basic session plan, you'll see small symbols in the margin. Each symbol stands for a different kind of option. When you see a symbol, it means that kind of option is offered for that step. Turn to the options section (which can be found immediately following the Repro Resources for each session), look for the category indicated by the symbol, and you'll see that option explained.

Let's say you have a small group, mostly guys who get bored if they don't keep moving. You'll want to keep an eye out for three kinds of options: Small Group, Mostly Guys, and Extra Action. As you read the basic session, you might spot symbols that tell you there are Small Group options for Step 1 and Step 3—maybe a different way to play a game so that you don't need big teams, and a way to cover several Bible passages when just a few kids are looking them up. Then you see symbols telling you that there are Mostly Guys options for Step 2 and Step 4—perhaps a substitute activity that doesn't require too much self-disclosure, and a case study guys will relate to. Finally you see symbols indicating Extra Action options for Step 2 and Step 3—maybe an active way to get kids' opinions instead of handing out a survey, and a way to act out some verses instead of just looking them up.

After reading the options, you might decide to use four of them. You base your choices on your personal tastes and the traits of your group that you think are most important right now. **Custom Curriculum** offers you more options than you'll need, so you can pick your current favorites and plug others into future meetings if you like.

(3) *Use the checklist.* Once you've picked your options, keep track of them with the simple checklist that appears at the end of each option section (just before the start of the next session plan). This little form gives you a place to write down the materials you'll need, too—since they depend on the options you've chosen.

(4) *Get your stuff together.* Gather your materials; photocopy any Repro Resources (reproducible student sheets) you've decided to use. And . . . you're ready!

The Custom Curriculum Challenge

Your kids are fortunate to have you as their leader. You see them not as a bunch of generic teenagers, but as real, live, unique kids. You care whether you really connect with them. That's why you're willing to take a few extra minutes to tailor your meetings to fit.

It's a challenge to work with real, live kids, isn't it? We think you deserve a standing ovation for taking that challenge. And we pray that **Custom Curriculum** helps you shape sessions that shape lives for Jesus Christ and His kingdom.

—*The Editors*

Opportunity, Not Difficulty!
by Fran and Jill Sciacca

If you're honest with yourself, most likely you will confess that teaching a Sunday school class or leading a youth group meeting on what different churches believe will be about as easy as pushing a chain! Many of us in youth ministry are very adept at "doctrine dodging" or "polite postponement" ("Let me answer that question near the end of the session"). We dodge questions because of the difficulty associated with subjects that tend to generate a lot of heat, but very little light. On top of that, if you were to solicit a list of the top ten topics to avoid in a Sunday school class or youth group meeting, right behind theology would be denominationalism. So how is it, in the sovereignty of God, that you have been called to teach a class that contains both?!

On the other hand, you may be experiencing a sense of exhilaration at the opportunity to finally point out the folly of the Christians whose cars don't happen to be parked in your church's lot each week. You may see this as your chance to teach the "truth" of *your* denomination amidst a host of misled saints! Obviously, neither of these extremes is true, nor is it productive. In fact, the quickest way to alienate any teenager is to attack or poke fun at what's dear to him or her—be it music, sports, his or her church, or a *friend's* church. Your goal should be to use this excellent curriculum to educate yourself. Then you can educate your group regarding major denominations, their differences and distinctives.

In an age when many young people have been cut off from their past due to divorce and other circumstances, *"They're Not Like Us!"* affords an excellent opportunity to teach them about the history of the family of God as it grew and established itself in different denominations, doctrines, traditions, and practices. Understanding what we believe and why provides a sense of belonging and purpose—two tremendous needs of today's teens.

"They're Not Like Us!" is designed to be a "denominational defuser" that will guide you and your group members to a better appreciation and admiration of God's creative tapestry of reconciled sinners known as the Church. At a time as perilous as the present, God's people need to understand and appreciate one another. *"They're Not Like Us!"* can help cultivate a spirit of cooperation without compromise among the generation that constitutes the future of Christianity on this continent.

Having spent nearly two decades teaching Bible every day to high school students from over 120 churches, Jill and I believe that we have a few insights that you will find encouraging and enlightening. Here are a few things to ponder as you prepare to teach *"They're Not Like Us!"*

A Foundational Focus

In a classic passage on divisions within the church at Corinth, Paul lays out what must be understood as a crucial principle in denominationalism—namely, that the ultimate worth of any spiritual endeavor is only as good as its foundation.

"By the grace God has given me, I laid a foundation as an expert builder, and someone else is building on it. But each one should be careful how he builds. For no one can lay any foundation other than the one already laid, which is Jesus Christ. If any man builds on this foundation using gold, silver, costly stones, wood, hay, or straw, his work will be shown for what it is, because the Day will bring it to light. It will be revealed with fire, and the fire will test the quality of each man's work. If what he has built survives, he will receive his reward. If it is burned up, he will suffer loss; he himself will be saved, but only as one escaping through the flames" (I Corinthians 3:10-15).

The Corinthian church had succumbed to the temptation of setting themselves apart from one another and were virtually coming apart at the seams because they wanted to form little factions based on whose teaching they agreed with! Sound familiar? Paul's exhortation to them is not merely cultural, because it is intrinsically bound to the evaluation of all believers at the end of the age. Quite simply, Paul advises the Corinthians to focus on the foundation first, and the ministers second. He emphasizes the fact that only one foundation exists, a truth well worth building on as you prepare to teach *"They're Not Like Us!"*

Your group members need to know that the crucial question of any denomination or body of believers is whether or not Jesus Christ is at the center. What or who is esteemed? If it is the teaching of some person rather than the Person of Jesus, then the foundation is faulty no matter how attractive the rest of the fellowship appears. It is significant that Paul never sought anything for himself along the lines of notoriety. In fact, he defined his mission by saying, "When I came to you, brothers, I did not come with eloquence or superior wisdom as I proclaimed to you the testimony about God. For I resolved to know nothing while I was with you except Jesus Christ and him crucified" (I Corinthians 2:1, 2).

Paul preached the foundation of Jesus Christ and built his ministry from there. A foundation holds up a structure. If the structure is doing its job, it will be holding forth the foundation. Help your group members develop this critical perspective for evaluating other denominations and variations of the faith that populate our planet. Teach them to ask questions and study other denominations rather than pronouncing quick and final judgments. Is Jesus Christ the focus and foundation of this church, or is someone or something else being exalted?

Organism More Than Organizations

A second principle that the Apostle Paul stood firmly upon and sought to perpetuate was that the church of Jesus Christ is *not* primarily an institution. It is a living, changing, growing organism. In fact, the one metaphor that Paul uses more than any other to describe the church is the "body of Christ." Look carefully at these statements in Scripture:

"Just as each of us has one body with many members, and these members do not all have the same function, so in Christ we who are many form one body, and each member belongs to all the others" (Romans 12:4, 5).

"The body is a unit, though it is made up of many parts; and though all its parts are many, they form one body. So it is with Christ. For we were all baptized by one Spirit into one body—whether Jews or Greeks, slave or free—and we were all given the one Spirit to drink" (I Corinthians 12:12, 13).

"Let the peace of Christ rule in your hearts, since as members of one body you were called to peace. And be thankful" (Colossians 3:15).

The significance is obvious: we are related to one another on a level that transcends biology and pedigree. We are each *part* of Jesus Christ and therefore, in a very real sense, we are part of one another. This is not just sound theology; it is reality! The people down the street, across the country, or around the globe who genuinely confess Christ are an integral part of a larger whole to which we also belong. And we are not merely "connected," we are dependent upon one another. God has carefully and creatively arranged each part of His church to function together to accomplish His purposes in the world. Paul's use of the metaphor "body" is not merely an insightful concept. Together, we are Christ's voice, His hands, His heart, and His eyes. It is a sobering truth!

Help your kids see themselves as an integral part of this larger, living whole (I Corinthians 12:14-26). Young people need to know that in spite of denominational distinctions, there exists just one essential body of believers in this world that is known in God's Word as "the body of Christ." Your kids must see that though we often mistakenly categorize and separate ourselves denominationally, we really do need one another. We are not merely on the same team; Paul says we are the same body! Fortunately, young people seem more accepting of this truth than many adults. Young people tend to be more devoted to a "vision" (the body of believers) than to details (who's "right" and "wrong").

More Than Good Intentions

In an era when polls are considered to be the arbiters of truth, your kids need to understand that although the body of Christ knows no boundary, any endeavor claiming to be in fellowship with God must be judged by more than the number of warm bodies or depth of sentiment. I repeatedly emphasize to my students that it is possible to be *sincerely* wrong!

While there is a tremendous need for tolerance on issues that are secondary and acceptance of those whose heritage and worship styles don't work for us, there is also the absolute necessity for a standard by which to judge religious experience. It was this commitment to the standard of God's Word that set the Jews in Berea apart from those who mocked Paul in Thessalonica: "Now the Bereans were of more noble character than the Thessalonians, for they received the message with great eagerness and examined the Scriptures every day to see if what Paul said was true" (Acts 17:11).

The measure of dedication one has to an idea cannot be a standard by which to judge its validity. Frequently, young people fail to distinguish between mere sentiment and commitment. Here is where balance belongs—in the need to look beyond the "vision" to details and distinctives, to discern right from wrong, heresy from truth. It is possible to have very strong feelings about something that is not true. Intensity of feelings never *makes* something true. This is important simply because in the midst of a discussion such as denominationalism, one has to remind himself or herself that everyone can't be right about everything! "Everyone" includes me, you, and all of your group members.

The more serious truth is that God holds *me* responsible to make *my* judgments upon the basis of the best understanding I can muster of His Word. My feelings about an issue can never substitute for a thorough understanding of what God Himself has said about it. This is as true of a mode of baptism as it is of the veneration of Mary and the saints. My standard must be the same as the Bereans—Scripture itself. Emphasize the importance of studying and regularly seeking to understand the Word of God above all things.

Don't Underestimate Your Audience

Very early in the twentieth century, a massive revival broke out in Wales. Thousands were turned to Christ in a span of just a few months. Taverns closed because they had no customers. Traveling theater groups stopped performing because people were too busy sharing the Gospel and worshiping to come to their shows. Some cities did not record a single arrest during this period. The most sobering fact about this intense movement of God was that the majority of those ministering were between the ages of sixteen and twenty-six!

In the midst of a seemingly hopeless season for helping today's youth culture, Jill and I are seeing a growing number of people who work with high school students talk of strange rumblings among their groups. There appears to be a discontent with the status-quo Christianity that characterizes many of our churches. Increasing numbers of Christian young people are hungering for depth and devotion. They speak of sacrifice and authenticity rather than success and affluence. Christian leaders such as Chuck Colson and Os Guinness have spoken and written about the need for a wholesale revival in our land. Is it possible that if such a movement of God is to come, it might come from among the likes of those who sit before you each Sunday?

If God does bring revival to our land, it will certainly not be constrained to the boundaries set by denominationalism. It will be a movement of the Spirit across the sinews of the body of Christ. Perhaps the part you will play by teaching *"They're Not Like Us!"* will be far more significant than you ever imagined! Carry on!

Fran and Jill Sciacca have been involved with youth ministry for nearly two decades. Fran is a high school teacher. Jill has a degree in journalism and sociology and is a full-time homemaker and a free-lance writer/editor. She has written for Discipleship Journal *and* Decision *magazine, and has served on the editorial team for the* Youth Bible *(Word). Fran and Jill coauthored* Lifelines *(Zondervan), an award-winning Bible study series for high schoolers. Fran is the author of the best-selling Bible study,* To Walk and Not Grow Weary *(NavPress), as well as* Generation at Risk *(Moody), and* Wounded Saints *(Baker).*

Publicity Clip Art

The images on these two pages are designed to help you promote this course within your church and community. Feel free to photocopy anything here and adapt it to fit your publicity needs. The stuff on this page could be used as a flier that you send or hand out to kids—or as a bulletin insert. The stuff on the next page could be used to add visual interest to newsletters, calendars, bulletin boards, or other promotions. Be creative and have fun!

Why Are There So Many Different Churches to Choose From?

Shouldn't all Christians believe the same thing? What do Baptists believe that Lutherans disagree with? What's the difference between a Catholic church and a Greek Orthodox church? How should I treat people from other denominations? Is there anything that *all* Christians agree on? Join us for a new series called *"They're Not Like Us!"* as we tackle these and other tough questions concerning what different churches believe.

Who:

When:

Where:

Questions? Call:

"They're Not Like Us!"

"They're Not Like Us!"

Which church is right?

Ever wonder why other churches worship the way they do?

Hear ye, hear ye!

A reformed church?

SESSION 1

So Many Flavors
(Why Different Churches Believe Different Things)

YOUR GOALS FOR THIS SESSION:
Choose one or more
☐ To help kids become familiar with some basic beliefs of different Christian denominations.
☐ To help kids understand that there is a proper diversity among Christians in some religious practices and non-essential beliefs.
☐ To help kids accept believers of other denominations as Christian brothers and sisters.
☐ Other _____

Your Bible Base:

Acts 6:1-4; 11:1-3, 19-21; 15:1-6, 36-41; 18:24-28; 19:1-5
I Corinthians 3:3-9
Philippians 1:14-18
III John 9, 10

C U S T O M C U R R I C U L U M

STEP 1

What Do You Know?

(Needed: Copies of Repro Resource 1, pencils, prizes [optional])

Welcome your group members as they arrive. Explain that you're starting a series on denominations. Ask: **What is a denomination?** You're not necessarily looking for a "right" answer here; instead, you're looking for kids' impressions of what a denomination is. (Our best definition is "a subgroup of Christians that worships in a particular way or believes particular doctrines.")

Then ask: **How many different denominations can you name?** See how many examples your group members can come up with in one minute. Examples might include Baptist, Methodist, Catholic, Episcopalian, Presbyterian, and Evangelical Free.

Hand out copies of "This Is a Test" (Repro Resource 1) and pencils. Let kids work in pairs or small groups to complete the sheet. Emphasize that this quiz is just for fun; if group members don't know the answer to a question, they should guess. Give kids a few minutes to complete the sheet. When everyone is finished, go through the answers as a group. You might want to award prizes to the pair or group that came up with the most correct answers. Use the following information to supplement your discussion of the sheet.

1. *What is the method of baptism favored by Baptists?* (b—Dunking.) The fancy term is "immersion," which involves dunking a person underwater as a symbol of Christ's burial and resurrection. Many other churches use sprinkling. If there were any churches that used drowning, they've died out by now.

2. *Where does the name "Presbyterian" come from?* (b—The Greek word *presbuteroi*, for the elders who govern the church.)

3. *What does the "method" of the Methodist denomination refer to?* (a—John Wesley's system of spiritual development.) John Wesley, the supposed founder of the Methodist group, tried to get Anglicans to be more serious about their faith, so he developed a "method" of personal devotion and small group fellowship. The term "Methodists" was first used by others, in derision.

4. *Why are Lutherans named for Martin Luther?* (b—The Lutheran church follows Luther's approach to the Scriptures.) Martin Luther led the first major break from the Roman Catholic church in the 1500s.

5. *Which of the following statements is true?* (b—Episcopalians are pretty much the same as Anglicans.) "Episcopal" comes from the Greek

word for "bishop"; it refers to the denomination's system of church government. You might say that Episcopalians are "American Anglicans"—they do belong to the worldwide Anglican church. By the way, Plymouth Brethren are named for their origins in Plymouth, England. They may drive any car they want. The Evangelical Free church is free to attend. The name refers to its style of worship. The Reformed church goes back to the Reformation led by John Calvin in the 1500s.

  6. *Where does the name "Mennonites" come from?* (d—A man named Menno.) Menno Simons was a Dutch church leader who inspired the founding of the Mennonite church.

  7. *Which of the following denominations promotes speaking in tongues?* (c—Assemblies of God.) This is the largest of several Pentecostal denominations, which promote the use of tongues as an evidence of the Spirit's filling.

  8. *Of Swedish Baptists, Roman Catholics, Greek Orthodox, and Dutch Reformed, which group has the tastiest fellowship dinners?* You're on your own here.

  9. *What is the largest group in Christendom within the United States?* (a—The Roman Catholic church.) The Roman Catholic church has approximately 58.5 million members. The Southern Baptist Convention has about 15 million members (though Baptists of all kinds number about 31 million). The United Methodist church has about 8.9 million members.

  10. *If you hear people talking about sprinkling babies, meetings of "the session," and the teachings of John Calvin, where are you most likely to be?* (a—A Presbyterian church.) Babies are baptized by sprinkling, "the session" is the ruling group of elders, and John Calvin is the Reformer whose teachings have informed most Presbyterian theology.

STEP 2

Where It All Began

(Needed: Bibles, chalkboard and chalk or newsprint and marker)

Say: **Sometimes these denominations seem ridiculous. I mean, why do we have so many divisions? Why can't all Christians agree? Why can't we have unity—like they had in the early church?**

Unity? In the early church? Not exactly. Almost from the start, there were disagreements and divisions. And—sur-

prise—not all of these divisions were bad.

Assign the following Scripture passages for kids to look up and have ready to read: Acts 6:1-4; Acts 11:1-3; Acts 11:19-21; Acts 15:1-6; Acts 15:36-41; Acts 18:24-28; Acts 19:1-5; I Corinthians 3:3-9; Philippians 1:14-18; III John 9, 10.

Go through the passages quickly, not mulling over details, but simply getting a feel for the climate of the early church. Use the following questions and information to supplement your discussion of the passages.

Acts 6:1-4

Ask: **What was the problem here?** (Greek-speaking widows were complaining that they were being discriminated against.) This was probably a cultural division. At this time, all Christians were Jews. However, the Hebrew-speaking Jews would have been more conservative and local to Jerusalem. Greek-speaking Jews were probably more progressive; they may have been out-of-towners who stayed in Jerusalem after Pentecost, and thus had no family support.

Was the result of this division good or bad? (It was probably good. Deacons were appointed to handle the problem.)

Acts 11:1-3

Ask: **What was the problem here?** (Peter had preached to Gentiles, something the more conservative Jewish Christians had a problem with.) In order to understand the scandal here, you must remember that Gentiles were "unclean" according to their understanding of Old Testament law.

Acts 11:19-21

Ask: **Who was "speak[ing] to Greeks"—that is, to Gentiles?** ("Men from Cyprus and Cyrene.")

Why weren't men from Jerusalem doing this? Wasn't Jerusalem the center of the church? (Yes, but people had scattered as a result of persecution. In addition, the Jerusalem believers seemed to be hesitant about opening up to Gentiles.) A very important point to remember here is that geography matters. Write "Geography" on the board. First, persecution scattered Christians out of Jerusalem. Was this good or bad? Bad in one way, but the scattering meant that the Gospel was going to new places like Cyprus and Cyrene. The new Jewish believers from Cyprus and Cyrene then had no problem going to Antioch to preach to non-Jews. Cypriot Jews were doing what Jerusalem Jews would not do.

Today there are many geographically based groups or denominations (Swedish Baptist, Greek Orthodox, African Methodist Episcopal, etc.). It's likely that they can reach their particular cultures in ways that other churches cannot.

Acts 15:1-6

Ask: **What was the problem?** (Some people were saying that Gentile converts had to "become Jews" in order to become Christians.

Paul insisted that this was not necessary.) This was a major dispute that plagued Paul throughout his ministry. The "Judaizers," who insisted that Gentile Christians convert to Judaism and follow Jewish law, were believers in Christ. But they had a major disagreement with Paul over the nature of Christianity. Paul seems to have "won" in the long run.

Acts 15:36-41

Ask: **What was the problem here?** (Barnabas wanted to give a second chance to John Mark, the deserter. Paul refused.)

Who was right? (Who knows? Maybe both.)

Was the result good or bad? (Perhaps it was good, since it resulted in two missionary teams being formed.)

Acts 18:24-28

Ask: **What was the problem with Apollos's teaching?** (He knew only the baptism of John—that is, he preached that people needed to repent, but he probably didn't have the full awareness of Jesus' sacrificial death. He emphasized a *part* of the truth.)

Why do you think Apollos had this problem? (Perhaps he was out of touch with recent events. He may have been studying in Alexandria while Jesus was fulfilling the preaching of John the Baptist.)

Acts 19:1-5

Ask: **What was the problem?** (The Ephesians had heard a partial gospel, based on John's baptism. As Priscilla and Aquila had done with Apollos, Paul explained the way of God more thoroughly.) Denominations develop at different paces in different places. There were three or four "Reformation" movements that broke from the Catholic church—Luther's took hold in Germany, Calvin's in France and Switzerland, while there were ongoing rustlings of Anglican Reformers in England and Anabaptists in Central Europe. Like Apollos and the Ephesians, these Reformers developed independently of others, though their teachings were parallel to the others. Many denominations are the result of *history*, how things developed at a particular time. Write "History" on the board.

1 Corinthians 3:3-9

Ask: **What was the problem?** (Christians in Corinth were breaking into factions, following certain leaders.)

How did Paul respond to this problem? (He emphasized the teamwork of the various leaders.)

Do you think it was wrong for the Corinthians to admire the work of one leader more than that of another? (Probably not. The problem came in the division. When one group claimed superiority over another, that was a problem.)

Philippians 1:14-18

Ask: **Who was preaching while Paul was in prison?** (Apparently there were other preachers who didn't like Paul. They may have puffed up their own credentials and tried to "outpreach" Paul.)

What was Paul's response to them? (He was just pleased that the Gospel was being preached.)

How might Paul's attitude be a model for our attitude toward other denominations? (We may disagree with others' style, or even their motives, but we can support them if they preach the true Gospel of Christ.)

III John 9, 10

Ask: **What was the problem here?** (Diotrephes had an attitude problem. He was probably the leader of a house church, and he was shunning other Christians.)

How can we avoid this problem in our attitude toward other denominations? (We can remain humble, while still clinging to our understanding of the Truth. We can have fellowship with others and "agree to disagree" on points that are not essential matters of Christian faith.)

Ask: **Based on what we've read, what other reasons are there for Christians to have different groups, different beliefs, and different denominations? We have Geography and History written down. What else could we say?** Write the best of your group members' answers on the board. If no one mentions them, suggest these two reasons: "Disagreements" and "Personality Conflicts."

God Is . . . /We Are . . .

(Needed: Copies of Repro Resource 2, pencils)

Have kids form small groups. Ask each group to choose a number from 1 to 4 and a letter from A to D. The groups may duplicate a number or a letter, but you should not have two groups with the same letter-number combination. Based on the letters and numbers that the groups choose, you will assign each of them a statement about God and a statement about a church congregation. The groups will then make plans to form a denomination based on those statements.

The statements are as follows:

Statements about God
1. God is a shepherd.
2. God is a rock.
3. God is love.
4. God is holy.

Of course all of these statements are true, but each group should emphasize its own statement and forget about the others.

Statements about the congregation
A. We are shy.
B. We are loud.
C. We like to move.
D. We like to think deep thoughts.

Whether or not a statement is true of the kids in that group, they are to make their plans for a denomination as if it is true.

Hand out copies of "Invent Your Own!" (Repro Resource 2) to each group. Give the groups a few minutes to complete the sheet based on their assigned statements. When everyone is finished, go through the sheet one section at a time, asking each group to share and explain its responses for that section.

Add two more points to your list on the board: "Emphasis about God" and "Personal Style." Then ask: **How do these two issues affect some of the denominations you know of?** (For instance, Presbyterians and Reformed folks tend to emphasize the sovereignty and election of God, while Methodists emphasize human free will. Both groups believe in all of these issues, but choose to emphasize certain ones in certain ways. Many conservative churches emphasize God's holiness and judgment, while some other churches emphasize His love and forgiveness. Anglicans emphasize a God-given leadership structure, while Baptists and Brethren emphasize the personal priesthood of each believer. Charismatics and Pentecostals tend to have lively, emotion-filled worship. Some other denominations, by contrast, appear to them to be "God's frozen people." Some people enjoy a highly structured liturgical worship service; others prefer to "go with the flow." Some like having a leader to tell them what to do; others prize their independence.)

Essentials

(Needed: Poster-making materials, tape)

Read aloud the following quote from Puritan teacher Richard Baxter: **"In essentials, unity. In non-essentials, liberty. In all things, charity."** Then ask group members to tell you what they think the quote means.

Ask: **What are the essentials of Christianity?** Suggest that

group members look up passages like John 14:6; Acts 4:12; Ephesians 2:8-10; and Hebrews 11:6. These passages all point to one primary Christian essential: faith in Jesus Christ as the only way to God. Scripture is clear that there is no other path, other than Jesus, and that our good works cannot save us. Of course, this faith implies a belief in a caring God who wants to be found by those who seek Him (Hebrews 11:6).

Ask: **What are some non-essential matters that Christians care about?** [NOTE: It's not that these matters aren't important; it's just that they're not at the center of our faith.] (Non-essential matters might include mode of baptism, what happens at the Lord's Supper, forms of church leadership, style of singing, speaking in tongues, and beliefs about the end times.)

Have kids form groups of three. Hand out poster-making materials to each group. Instruct each group to make a poster that illustrates the Richard Baxter quote you read earlier. Group members may add any drawings or other words to their posters that they want. For instance, they might list some specific essentials and non-essentials of the Christian. Or they might write down some specific ways to show "charity" (or love). Give kids a few minutes to work. When everyone is finished, have each group display and explain its poster. Then display all of the posters around your meeting area.

STEP 5

Bridge-Building

As you wrap up the session, say: **You probably know some Christians who belong to other denominations—perhaps some kids at school. How might you reach out to one of these people this week? Not to get them to come to this church or anything, but just to say, "I'm a Christian too." You might get into an interesting discussion about what the other person believes. If so, that's great. Or you may just say, "Praise God!" and go on your way. Regardless, try to make a connection like that this week.**

Close the session in prayer, asking God for the wisdom to hold to the essentials, while living in charity toward people of other denominations.

"THEY'RE NOT LIKE US!" REPRO RESOURCE 1

This Is a test

1. What is the method of baptism favored by Baptists?
  a. Sprinkling   c. Spitting
  b. Dunking   d. Drowning

2. Where does the name "Presbyterian" come from?
  a. The Latin term *pressus butus*, for "pressing into service"
  b. The Greek word *presbuteroi*, for the elders who govern the church
  c. The English word *presby*, for the kind of hat often worn by church founder John Knox
  d. The computer term *pre-byte*, for the early calculators that were used to count the offering

3. What does the "method" of the Methodist denomination refer to?
  a. John Wesley's system of spiritual development
  b. Its form of collegial church government
  c. The acting technique used by nineteenth-century star Sarah Bernhardt, the denomination's most famous member
  d. A code name for Methuselah, because most Methodists are very old

4. Why are Lutherans named for Martin Luther?
  a. They worship him as a god.
  b. The Lutheran church follows Luther's approach to the Scriptures.
  c. The Lutheran church was started in a country where he was king.
  d. Early church leaders thought he had a cool name, but didn't want to call themselves Martinians.

5. Which of the following statements is true?
  a. Plymouth Brethren are forbidden to drive Fords.
  b. Episcopalians are pretty much the same as Anglicans.
  c. It actually costs $10 to join an Evangelical Free Church.
  d. To join the Reformed Church, you must have served time in prison.

6. Where does the name "Mennonites" come from?
  a. The denomination's practice of having women worship in the morning and "men at night"
  b. The teaching that men are superior to women
  c. From the Latin word *mens*, which indicates an emphasis on the mind
  d. A man named Menno

7. Which of the following denominations promotes speaking in tongues?
  a. Nazarenes   c. Assemblies of God
  b. Conservative Baptists   d. Berlitzians

8. Of Swedish Baptists, Roman Catholics, Greek Orthodox, and Dutch Reformed, which group has the tastiest fellowship dinners?

9. What is the largest group in Christendom within the United States?
  a. The Roman Catholic Church   c. The United Methodist Church
  b. The Southern Baptist Convention   d. The Multiplistic Offerings Church

10. If you hear people talking about sprinkling babies, meetings of "the session," and the teachings of John Calvin, where are you most likely to be?
  a. A Presbyterian church   c. A child psychologist's office
  b. An Orthodox church   d. Heaven

"THEY'RE NOT LIKE US!" REPRO RESOURCE 2

Invent Your Own!

Statement about God: _____

Statement about the Congregation: _____

Music
Will your worship services include singing? Why or why not?

If your worship service includes singing, what kind of songs will you sing? Why?

Are there any specific songs you would want to include in your hymnal? If so, what are they?

What will the members of your denomination do as they sing? (Stand? Sway? Dance? Pray? Jog?)

Preaching
Will your worship service include a sermon? Why or why not?

What kind of preaching or teaching would you prefer?

Organization
What sort of church leadership will your denomination have? (Ordained pastors? Elders? Deacons? Democracy? A pope?) *[Remember to answer the questions on the basis of the statements you've been given.]*

Other
What other activities will be included as part of your denomination? (Fellowship dinners? Outreach programs? A bowling team?) Explain.

How would a church in your denomination relate to the community around it? (Would it be heavily involved in community affairs? Would it separate itself from the community? Would it be evangelistic? Would it be judgmental? Would it get involved in local politics?) Explain.

What would a church youth group be like in your denomination? Explain.

OPTIONS

SESSION ONE

Step 1
Designate four areas of the room as "a," "b," "c," and "d." Rather than having kids fill out Repro Resource 1, read each of the questions on the sheet aloud. Have each group member indicate his or her response by moving to the appropriate area in the room. Ask volunteers to explain why they answered as they did.

Step 5
Close the session with an ice cream-tasting contest. You'll need to bring in several containers of different flavors of ice cream. Cover the containers so that kids can't see the labels. Number each container. Hand out paper, pencils, and spoons. Have kids file past the containers one at a time, sampling each flavor of ice cream. Then have them write down their guesses as to what each flavor is. After everyone has had a chance to sample all flavors, reveal the correct answers. Close the session by letting kids finish the rest of the ice cream. Use this activity to serve as a reminder of the many different "flavors" of Christianity.

Step 3
Rather than having kids form small groups to work on Repro Resource 2, let your group members pick several random letter-number combinations and work together to discuss each "denomination" option. You won't need to make copies of the Repro Resource. You can simply ask the questions from the sheet for each "denomination" you create. To keep this activity from becoming redundant, designate one person each time to be the decision-maker in case there are differences of opinion. Also be aware that throughout this series, kids are probably going to have questions about how their own church fits into the picture. During this first session, they may not be ready to ask bold questions, but their concerns are likely to come up as they design "new" kinds of churches. Listen for clues to unexpressed confusion or unasked questions.

Step 5
Before you send the members of your small group out into the world in search of other "brands" of Christians, you may want to make sure that they know they have the support of each other. One thing you can do is create pins or buttons to wear, or perhaps provide them with matching articles of clothing (caps, T-shirts, etc.) that would help them identify with each other before they begin to try to identify with people they don't know as well. If other kids see a few people displaying the same kind of jewelry or clothing, they may feel they are missing out on something. (Perhaps they will discover they *are*, and will give church a chance.)

Step 2
Have kids form teams. Assign each team one or more of the passages listed in Step 2. Also give each team the appropriate questions from the session to answer regarding its passage. After a few minutes, have each team explain its passage and answer its assigned questions for the rest of the group. If teams don't mention it, emphasize the role that geography and history played in the formation of denominations. Then pick up the session plan with the last paragraph in Step 2.

Step 5
Have kids form small groups. Instruct each group to come up with two brief roleplays—one that demonstrates the *wrong* way to approach someone from a different denomination and then one that demonstrates the *right* way. The wrong-approach scenarios may be exaggerated and humorous, but the right-approach scenrios should be serious. After a few minutes, have each group perform its scenarios. Close the session in prayer, asking God to help your group members live in charity toward people of other denominations.

OPTIONS

SESSION ONE

HEARD IT ALL BEFORE

Step 1
If your kids think they've heard it all before when it comes to denominations, add a little excitement to the quiz on Repro Resource 1. At the beginning of the quiz, give each person ten jelly beans (or some other kind of candy). Explain that for each question on the quiz, kids may risk any or all of their jelly beans. If they get the correct answer, they win the number of jelly beans that they risked; if they don't get the correct answer, they lose that number of jelly beans. Rather than having kids fill in Repro Resource 1, read each question aloud and let kids indicate their responses by raising their hands. See who has the most jelly beans at the end of the quiz.

Step 3
Have kids form two teams. Give each team five minutes to list as many different denominations as it can think of. When time is up, have each team read its list. Award one point for each denomination, two points for each denomination not mentioned by the other team. Give prizes to the winning team, if you desire. Then move on to the "statements about God/statements about the congregation" activity.

LITTLE BIBLE BACKGROUND

Step 1
Group members with little knowledge of the Bible probably have even less knowledge of church history and doctrinal differences between denominations. It will do little good to discuss all sorts of other churches if your kids know nothing about their own church. The quiz on Repro Resource 1 should be all right because of its light tone, but it should be followed immediately with a discussion of what *your* church believes. If it turns out that the plan of salvation is new to many of your members, matters such as baptism and history should be postponed. Spend your time focusing on what is most important.

Step 2
The whirlwind tour through the Book of Acts is likely to be too "windy" for group members with little previous understanding of what is taking place. Rather than bouncing from passage to passage, it will be better for you to do a lot of summarizing as to what problems the early church faced. From time to time, have your group members get personally involved by looking up a passage; but you will probably need to scale back considerably on the amount of reading and responding that is required in the session as written.

FELLOWSHIP & WORSHIP

Step 1
As group members arrive, have soft instrumental music playing. Gather kids together for a short time of worship. Play a recording of (or have kids sing) "Jesus Loves Me." Ask group members to talk about what Jesus' love means to them. Close your worship time in prayer, praising God for His love. Then say: **There are many different ways in which people react and respond to the truth of God's love, and there are many different ways of worshiping Him. We're going to take a look at a few of those different worship styles in this series.**

Step 4
After kids have completed their posters, take them to an area which you've prepared for them to make a "gutter banana split." You'll need a clean plastic gutter, several different kinds of ice cream and toppings, and spoons. Give kids an opportunity to make a giant banana split in the gutter; then let them dig in. As kids are flailing about in chocolate syrup and whipped cream, point out that they started with a wide variety of ingredients, and put them all together to form one pretty good whole. Similarly, there are many different types of worship, but all believers come together to form the whole body of Christ.

OPTIONS

SESSION ONE

 **MOSTLY GIRLS**

 **MOSTLY GUYS**

 **EXTRA FUN**

Mostly Girls

Step 2
After your girls have read and discussed the Scripture passages listed, say: **Paul wrote many letters to churches that he had a relationship with. Now we're going to write some letters of our own.** Have each of your girls identify a "problem" they see in the church today, whether in your own church or the church universal. Instruct your girls to write a letter to the people who may be involved in the problem, addressing their concerns and fears; let them know that they don't have to come up with answers. After a few minutes, ask volunteers to read their letters.

Step 3
For the opening activity in Step 3, replace Statement C about the congregation with the following: "We believe in equality of the sexes." After the activity, ask: **How do you think your church would feel about women having equal status as men? How do you think God feels about it?** This could be a hot topic for discussion. Field questions and comments as necessary.

Mostly Guys

Step 3
When you get to Repro Resource 2, let your guys design an all-male church. The statement about God should be "God is male" and the statement about the congregation should be "No women allowed." Work through the questions on the sheet. Afterward, ask: **What would you think about having all-male and all-female churches? What would be the potential advantages? What would be the shortcomings?** After discussing the shortcomings, ask: **How do you think women feel when they try to worship in a place that seems to put more emphasis on guys than on girls? What can you do to help keep this from becoming a problem in our church?**

Step 5
Try to be more specific about the challenge to identify and speak to other Christians at school. (Guys sometimes need incentives and challenges spelled out for them.) Rather than asking guys to find one church attender this week, designate Thursday (or any other school day) as "Fellow Christian Identification Day." Have the guys in your group compete to see who can compile the longest list of other Christians at school. In each case, your guys should find out what church (and denomination) the other person goes to. At your next meeting, see who has listed the most different Christian peers and how extensive a list of churches and denominations you can compile.

Extra Fun

Step 1
Before you begin the quiz on Repro Resource 1, create a quiz to see how much your group members know about their own church. Find a copy of the church constitution, information about its denominational ties, and so forth. Ask kids to identify the entire official name of the church, the name of the pastor, what kind of church government it has, what missions it supports, what it does to attract new people, and anything else that seems relevant. Although the subject is a bit dry, keep the quiz lighthearted by cheering correct answers and acting pained when kids don't know something they should about their own church. Food rewards (such as wrapped pieces of candy) for correct answers usually add to the fun level of any activity as well.

Step 3
After kids complete Repro Resource 2, ask them to consider starting a church that's based almost exclusively on "personal style." Each group member should create "The First Church of [the person's name]." Give kids time to come up with ways that their churches will be different than any others that currently exist. For example, at what time will the meetings take place? Many churches have baptistries, but what special rooms might your kids' churches have? What will their churches offer to get new people to attend? Explain that this should be a *fun* activity—not an actual church-building plan.

OPTIONS

SESSION ONE

Step 1
Before the session, record ID clips (station identifications) from as many different TV channels as possible. Play the tape for your group members; see how many clips they recognize. Then ask kids to list as many other TV channels as they can think of. Use this activity to introduce the topic of different denominations.

Step 3
Play recordings of several different hymns and Christian songs. Make sure that you include a variety of styles of music. Play some uptempo songs that encourage kids to clap their hands or tap their feet. Then play some slow songs that encourage kids to silently reflect on God. Afterward, discuss the different styles of worship employed by different denominations.

Step 1
Rather than using Repro Resource 1, try a shorter opener. Ask volunteers to share examples of times when they attended a worship service at a church of a different denomination from your church. Ask them to explain some of the differences between the two worship styles. Use group members' examples to lead in to the discussion in Step 2.

Step 2
Use only the Acts 11:19-21 and Acts 19:1-5 passages, emphasizing the role that geography and history played in the formation of denominations. In Step 3, use only the "God is love" and "God is holy" statements about God and only the "We are shy" and "We are loud" statements about the congregation.

Step 1
Rather than using Repro Resource 1, try a different opener. Ask volunteers to talk about some of the various ethnic cultures represented in their neighborhood. (If there are a variety of ethnic groups represented in your group, simply ask a few kids to talk about their cultures.) How does the Korean culture differ from the African-American culture? How does the Hispanic culture differ from the Polish (or German or Irish) culture? Use this discussion to introduce the topic of different denominations.

Step 3
Spend a few minutes finding out what preconceived notions your kids have concerning various denominations and Christian groups. Ask group members to call out the first things that come to mind when you mention terms like "Baptist," "Roman Catholic," "Charismatic," "Pentecostal," and so forth. After listening to kids' responses, lead in to a discussion of Richard Baxter's quote in Step 4.

OPTIONS

SESSION ONE

Step 2
Pair up your junior highers with high schoolers. Assign each pair one of the passages in Step 2. Instruct each pair to translate the problem faced by the early church into a modern-day dilemma. (For example, the widows being discriminated against in Acts 6:1-4 might be changed to modern-day divorcées.) The pair should look at how the early church addressed the issue and then suggest a solution for the modern-day scenario. After a few minutes, have each pair share what it came up with. Afterward, point out that human nature is much the same today as it was in the first century—and that God's Word still addresses our problems.

Step 3
Divide kids into two teams—a junior high team and a high school team. Assign each team the same letter-number combination; then let the teams make their plans to form a denomination. After a few minutes, have each team share what it came up with. Compare the junior highers' plan with the high schoolers' plan. Discuss any similarities and differences that you see. Point out that there are many things that affect our worship style, including age. If you have time, repeat the process, using a different letter-number combination.

Step 4
After reading the Richard Baxter quote, ask: **What are some practices of our church that might be considered "nonessential"? How do they differ from the practices of other denominations? How should we feel about such practices? Why?** Encourage several group members to offer their thoughts.

Step 5
As a group, brainstorm some ideas for bringing together young people from different churches (of various denominations) in your area. For example, you might plan a bowling party in which youth groups from different churches compete against each other. Whatever activity you plan, make sure that you include a time of fellowship to demonstrate to the kids that though they come from different denominations, they still have a common bond.

Date Used:

Approx. Time

Step 1: What Do You Know? _____
o Extra Action
o Heard It All Before
o Little Bible Background
o Fellowship & Worship
o Extra Fun
o Media
o Short Meeting Time
o Urban
Things needed:

Step 2: Where It All Began _____
o Large Group
o Little Bible Background
o Mostly Girls
o Short Meeting Time
o Combined Junior High/High School
Things needed:

Step 3: God Is . . ./We Are . . . _____
o Small Group
o Heard It All Before
o Mostly Girls
o Mostly Guys
o Extra Fun
o Media
o Urban
o Combined Junior High/High School
Things needed:

Step 4: Essentials _____
o Fellowship & Worship
o Extra Challenge
Things needed:

Step 5: Bridge-Building _____
o Extra Action
o Small Group
o Large Group
o Mostly Guys
o Extra Challenge
Things needed:

SESSION 2

The Big Three

(An Overview of Protestant, Catholic, and Orthodox Beliefs)

YOUR GOALS FOR THIS SESSION:
Choose one or more

☐ To help kids learn the basics of the history and distinctives of Protestantism, Catholicism, and Orthodoxy.

☐ To help kids understand some of the theological issues that brought these groups into being.

☐ To help kids determine the importance of those theological issues in their own lives.

☐ Other _____

Your Bible Base:

Ephesians 2:1-10

STEP 1

Pizza! Pizza!

(Needed: Chairs, pizzas [optional])

To begin the session, have kids form small groups. If possible, arrange the chairs in your meeting area to accommodate the small groups before the session. Pretend that your meeting room is a pizza parlor. Explain that each group is sitting at a "table," getting ready to order one pizza. The members of each group must decide what they want on their pizza—mushrooms, olives, sausage, anchovies, or whatever.

For one group, appoint a leader who will decide for the group what to order on the pizza. Instruct the members of another group to select a leader to decide what to order on their pizza. Make sure that at least one group is leaderless.

Give the groups a couple of minutes to decide; then take their orders. (If possible, go ahead and order real pizzas. If that's impossible, make it clear from the start that this is merely a game.)

Afterward, discuss the process of group decision making. Ask the leaderless group(s): **In your group, did one person take the lead or were all group members equally involved in the process?**

Did the majority rule or did your group seek the "lowest common denominator"—for instance, ordering a cheese pizza because one person doesn't like anything?

For those of you who ordered a half-and-half pizza, what does that indicate about your decision-making process?

After hearing all of the orders, do any of you wish that you were in a different group?

Ask the groups with leaders: **How did the appointed or elected leader affect the decision-making process?**

Then ask everyone: **What do you think this activity has to do with the topic of this series—denominations?** Field some of your kids' ideas. If no one mentions it, point out that churches are groups. In order to worship together, to conduct business together, to fellowship together, people need to decide certain things. In some cases, a leader—perhaps a pope or a bishop or a pastor—makes the key decisions for everyone else. In other cases, the church people decide for themselves.

New denominations are formed when a minority group says, "We hate mushrooms! We're going to order a separate pizza!" Sometimes those "mushrooms"—those disputed issues—are silly little *details*. But often they are major points of *doctrine*. Sometimes it's a *personality conflict* or a *leadership* question.

As Far As the East Is from the West

(Needed: Copies of Repro Resource 3, pencils)

Ask: **How are people in California different from people in Illinois? How are Texans different from New Yorkers?** There are no right or wrong answers here. You'll probably get a lot of generalizations; encourage kids to keep them kindhearted. The point is that people from different places act in different ways.

Why do these differences exist? (There might be root causes like weather, population density, pace of life, and history; but after a while, it just *is*. Californians become laid-back because they see everyone else being laid-back.)

Explain: **The same thing is true in the history of Christianity. For the first thousand years, there was one large, comprehensive church—though splinter groups arose from time to time. But Eastern churches developed different customs and practices from the Western church. The two churches were *officially united, but practically different*. For example, if today you went to a Catholic church in Chicago and a Catholic church in Brazil, they'd be similar, but they'd also have differences based on their geographical location.**

The official split took place in 1054, when the leader of the Western church tried to get the leader of the Eastern church to submit to his authority. When he refused, the Western leader excommunicated the Eastern leader—threw him out of the church—and the Eastern leader excommunicated the Western leader. Suddenly there were two churches—the Roman Catholic and the Eastern Orthodox.

So the *official* split occurred because of a leadership dispute—a personality conflict. But it really just expressed some basic geographical differences that had been causing friction for some time.

Hand out copies of "Different Strokes" (Repro Resource 3) and pencils. Encourage kids to take notes on the sheet while you talk (or at least try to dissuade them from turning the sheet into a paper airplane).

Explain: **Two major differences in these denominations are** probably the result of that initial "divorce." First is the issue of *leadership*. Catholics have a Pope and Eastern Orthodox churches do not. The Orthodox groups have a head patriarch who sort of runs the church, but he is considered "first among equals." He does not have the same amount of authority that the Pope has over Catholics. A second difference is that the Orthodox denomination seems to allow for geographical distinctions. Greek Orthodox, Russian Orthodox, Romanian Orthodox, and other local branches have been allowed to develop their own worship customs. These are all members of the larger Orthodox fellowship.

Other differences have occurred since the split. For instance, the Catholic church developed teachings regarding the celibacy of priests, the infallibility of the Pope, and purgatory, while Orthodox churches did not.

There are several other distinctives of Orthodox churches that should be noted. First, they have a strong tradition of mysticism. They emphasize the spirit more than the mind. How can a believer grow closer to the Lord? How can the church be united with God? How can we "pray without ceasing" as we live our lives? These are crucial questions for the Eastern Orthodox Church.

One element of this tradition is the practice of saying the "Jesus Prayer." Very simply, it's the repetition of the words, "Lord Jesus, be merciful to me a sinner," as you go through your day. If it truly comes from your heart, it's a way of grounding yourself in the love of God.

A second distinctive is the elaborate worship in Orthodox churches. In fact, the word "Orthodox" comes from the Greek for "proper worship." In Orthodox belief, Christianity is not just an individual thing; rather, each believer is part of the larger drama of salvation. That drama is played out in each worship service. To the uninformed, an Orthodox worship service may seem like a jumble of processions, incense, music, chants, and statues; but everything in the service means something. The whole service is intended to play out the Gospel.

One distinctive of Orthodox churches that Protestants find difficult to accept is their use of icons. Icons are basically statues or pictures of saints. They are used in public worship and personal devotion. As in Roman Catholic tradition, the saints are "venerated," or shown respect, but they're not supposed to take the place of God as the object of worship. The idea is that their spirits can continue to help us grow closer to God. Just as you might ask a respected pastor for advice on a spiritual matter, or you might ask a fellow believer to pray for you, so we can ask great Christians of the past for spiritual help—at least, that's what Orthodox teachings hold. In the Orthodox faith, the saints, as depicted in their icons, testify to worshipers about Christ.

STEP 3

Nailed to the Door

(Needed: Copies of Repro Resource 4, various trinkets)

Say: **I've got a great idea. Here's how we can raise money for _____** (fill in the blank with some youth group or church project, either real or potential).

Hold up a small piece of wood. Say: **See what this is? It's no ordinary piece of wood. The man who gave it to me said it was a piece of Jesus' cross! How much do you think we could sell this for?** Get a couple of responses.

Hold up four or five other trinkets. Ask group members to come up with "biblical identities" for them. For instance, you might have a string from Simon Peter's fishing net, a strap from John the Baptist's sandal, one of the pebbles that David *didn't* sling at Goliath, and so on.

Continue: **Oh, but these aren't just collectibles. They have spiritual power that still resides in them. They can solve your problems.**

Ask: **What do you think about my idea? Would we succeed in making money? Would it be a good thing to do? Why or why not?** (Would it succeed? Probably. Perhaps people are less gullible now, but look at the recent craze regarding crystals. Would it be a good thing to do? No. Obviously it focuses worship on objects rather than on God. No matter how good the cause is, we shouldn't stoop to such methods.)

Explain: **There was a time in the Roman Catholic church when this kind of thing was going on. To be fair, many modern Catholics are rather embarrassed about this time in their history. It was a period of great corruption. Later, the Catholic church took steps to clean up its act.**

But at the time, the church was building a cathedral in Rome and needed money, so all sorts of items were sold. One Reformer joked that if all of the "pieces of the cross" were assembled, you could make a hundred crosses.

Not only that, but some priests were doing what amounted to selling *forgiveness*. If a loved one had died, you could pay money to get him or her to God faster. These were called "indulgences."

Ask: **Do you see a problem with this line of thinking? If so, what is it?** (The whole notion of paying for one's sins with money is outrageous. To Protestant ears, the whole notion of paying for one's sins *at all* is unbiblical. That is, we are saved by God's grace, not by our money or our deeds. God's forgiveness is granted freely.)

Say: **One Catholic priest during this time also had problems with the Church's actions. His name was Martin Luther. When an indulgence seller came to town, Luther wrote up a list of ninety-five complaints against these practices, and he nailed the list to the door of the church in Wittenberg, Germany. A number of Germans supported Luther, and the Protestant Reformation was born. Over the next century, the Reformation spread throughout Europe. It was a political revolution and a social revolution, but it was also a religious revolution.**

Ask for two volunteers to present a brief skit. Hand out copies of "MTV Meets ML" (Repro Resource 4) to your volunteers. ("Zap" could be either male or female. "Luther," of course, should be male.) After giving your actors a minute or two to read through the script, have them perform the skit.

Afterward, explain: **One key issue of the Protestant Reformation was the one made by Luther in this sketch: *salvation by faith, not by works*. The Reformers objected to the strong Catholic emphasis on doing religious deeds or giving money in order to gain favor with God. According to one story, Luther was in Rome and visited the staircase that Jesus had supposedly climbed to see Pilate. As was the custom, he was climbing it on his knees, saying a prayer at each step. But a Bible verse kept going through his mind, "The righteous will live by faith" (Romans 1:17). As he neared the top, he began to realize that this ritual could never save him, but that he would receive eternal life only through faith in Jesus. As the story goes, he stopped, turned around, and went home.**

Another key issue was the *priesthood of the believer*. In the Catholic tradition, the priest was a necessary link between any individual Christian and God. The priest was the only one who could interpret Scripture properly or handle the sacraments. The Reformation brought out the idea that every Christian can deal with God directly, cutting out the "middle man."

Along with this was the *availability of Scripture*. The Catholic church had blocked any effort to translate the Bible into

the language of the people. At that time, the Bible was written in Latin, which almost no one except the priests spoke anymore. Luther translated it into modern German and, thanks to the newly invented printing press, people could suddenly read the Bible for themselves.

Ask: **How do Catholics and Protestants differ today?** Get as many responses as possible. Use the following information to supplement group members' responses.

• While the differences aren't as huge as they were at first, Catholics still tend to emphasize *good works* as essential to one's faith. Protestants emphasize the response of *faith* in making a personal decision to receive Christ. Both groups would agree that we are saved by God's grace, but they tend to differ on the human involvement and what that consists of.

• Catholics have the *unity* of one large worldwide organization, while Protestants have many splinter groups. This is a product of the Catholics' strong *central authority,* a superstructure of priests, bishops, and ultimately the Pope. Protestants, again, are more *individualistic*—basically, anyone with a strong opinion can start a denomination.

• Catholics also boast a *direct line of descent* from the New Testament church. (It should be noted that Orthodox churches make just as strong a claim to this.) But anyone would have to admit that there were some crazy twists and turns along the way. Most Protestants would say that *spiritual continuity* is more important. Does the church teach the authentic biblical Gospel?

STEP 4

Saved by Grace

(Needed: Bibles, paper, pencils, chalkboard and chalk or newsprint and marker)

Have kids reassemble into the groups they formed in Step 1. Distribute paper and pencils to each group. Instruct the groups to read Ephesians 2:1-10. Explain that you will write some questions on the board for the groups to discuss (and jot down answers to).

Write the following questions on the board:

• *The "you" in this text refers to all believers. With that in mind, what is our situation? What have we done?*

• *Where is the turning point in this passage?*

• *What does this passage say about God? What is He like? What does He do?*

• *Based on verses 8-10, what is the role of good works in the Christian's life?*

After a few minutes, go through the questions on the board, asking each group to share its responses. Use the following information to supplement your discussion of the questions.

• *The "you" in this text refers to all believers. With that in mind, what is our situation? What have we done?* (Our situation is that we're dead in transgressions and sins, objects of wrath, made alive by God, saved, raised up, seated with Christ, prepared to do good works. We have lived in sin, followed the ways of this world, gratified cravings, and followed our desires. But later we've done good works.)

• *Where is the turning point in this passage?* (Verse 4: "But because of his great love for us, God . . .")

• *What does this passage say about God? What is He like? What does He do?* (He is rich in mercy. He has made us alive. He saves us by grace. He's raised us with Christ and seated us with Him. He shows us riches of grace. He's kind to us. He prepares us as His workmanship.)

• *Based on verses 8-10, what is the role of good works in the Christian's life?* (Works are not irrelevant, but they enter late in the story of salvation. We are not saved by the works that we do. However, we are God's "good work." God has created us to be good. Having received His grace, we can begin to live as He intended all along.)

You may wish to conclude this session with your denomination's particular slant on the "good works" issue. You might want to make reference to James 2:26: "faith without deeds is dead."

In this material, we are not trying to pick on any particular religious tradition. The fact is that *many* churches and believers have forgotten the simple message of Ephesians 2 from time to time. Baptists, Catholics, Lutherans, Pentecostals, and many others may begin to rely on their good behavior to get them into God's good graces. That just puts everything backward. We need to rely solely on God's grace for entry into a relationship with Him, and then rely on His power for the good works that He wants us to do.

Close the session in prayer, thanking God for His grace and asking Him for power to live rightly.

DIFFERENT STROKES

"THEY'RE NOT LIKE US!"

REPRO RESOURCE 3

Orthodox and Catholic
The East-West split in 1054 was officially a leadership dispute, but it also arose from various differences that had been brewing for some time.

Differences
Leadership style—

Allowances for geographical differences—

Later adjustments in Catholic teaching—

Hallmarks of the Orthodox faith
Mysticism—

Elaborate worship—

Icons—

Catholic and Protestant
The Protestant Reformation was sparked in 1517 by Martin Luther's response to indulgence selling, but Europe was already a political, social, and religious powderkeg just waiting to explode.

Dividing issues
Salvation by faith, not works—

Priesthood of the believer—

Availability of Scripture—

Hallmarks of the Protestant faith
Emphasis on the individual's faith response to God—

Emphasis on spiritual continuity,
rather than on historical continuity—

Hallmarks of the Catholic faith
Living righteously with faith and good works is essential—

Unity/centralized leadership—

Continuity with the historical church—

"THEY'RE NOT LIKE US!" REPRO RESOURCE 4

MTV MEETS ML

ZAP: Hey, what's hoppin', dudes and dudettes? Welcome to the MTV History Hap. Hey, we got a special guest on the show today. Straight outta the history books and onto your screen. It's Doctor Martin Luther. *(To Luther)* 'Sup, G.
LUTHER: Uh, hello.
ZAP: Let me say first of all, my man, that I really dig that "I Have a Dream" speech. It is like *honkin'*. I mean, the man can communicate with a capital K, if you know what I'm sayin'.
LUTHER: I think you have me confused with someone else. I'm the one who said, "Here I stand. I can do no other."
ZAP: Run that by me again?
LUTHER: Here I stand. I can do no other. *(Gets no reaction from ZAP.)* I really liked it at the time.
ZAP: Here I stand?
LUTHER: They were trying to get me to recant, to give up my views about the changes that needed to be made in the church. I couldn't do it. That was where I stood, and there was nothing else I could do.
ZAP: Oh, I get it! Took a while, but I'm groovin' with ya now. You're the guy with the Protestant Restitution.
LUTHER: Reformation.
ZAP: So what exactly was the problem?
LUTHER: The problem was that the church was corrupt from top to bottom. The people had forgotten the simple message of God's grace, and they had substituted this whole system of doing religious works.
ZAP: Hey, I know people like that today!
LUTHER: Well, I guess there will always be people who try to work their way into God's favor. But that's not what the Bible says. It says that those who are righteous will live by *faith*.
ZAP: Hold on a second, Doctor M. Like this is blowin' my already fragile mind, OK? Are you tellin' me we don't have to be good?
LUTHER: Are you good?
ZAP: Good? I'm great! Just read a self-esteem book and I am floatin' away on myself.
LUTHER: But *morally*, are you good enough for God?
ZAP: Uh . . . well . . . if you put it that way . . . *morally* . . . uh . . . no.
LUTHER: Then join the club. None of us are good enough for God. But the good news is that God doesn't accept us on the basis of how good our behavior is. He accepts us on the basis of His grace and mercy in Jesus Christ. When we believe in Christ, then God can help us behave properly.
ZAP: Well, sorry to say it, big guy, but your fifteen seconds of fame are way gone. Back to our Smash-and-Grab Top Ten Countdown. See ya.

OPTIONS

SESSION TWO

Extra Action

Step 1
Have kids form two teams for some kind of a contest—perhaps a kickball or volleyball game. Rather than appointing a captain for each team, see how well team members do in organizing themselves. For instance, if you're playing kickball, how do teams determine their kicking order? How do they determine who plays what position? Pay particular attention to whether there's any disagreement or disgruntlement on the part of team members. Let kids play the game for a while. Afterward, use this activity to introduce the idea that leadership styles and methods of decision-making are two elements that distinguish certain denominations from each other.

Step 2
Begin Step 2 with a game of Red Rover. Have kids form two teams. Instruct the teams to stand several feet apart, facing each other. Have the members of each team spread out in a horizontal line, holding hands. To begin the game, one team will call to the other, "Red rover, red rover, let [the name of someone on the other team] come over." The person whose name is called will then run at the challenging team, trying to "split the team" by breaking the connection between two players. If the player succeeds, he or she gets to take one player from the challenging team back to his or her team; if the player fails, he or she must join the challenging team. Play several rounds of the game. Afterward, use the activity to introduce the splits that occurred in early church history.

Small Group

Step 1
If you don't have enough people to form groups for ordering pizzas, keep everyone in one group. Say: **I'm willing to buy pizza for this group—that is, if you can agree on what you want. But don't say anything out loud. I want you to write down your orders. If all of the orders are the same, then I'll assume we're in agreement and I'll place the order. If you don't agree, however, I might cause more hard feelings than goodwill by ordering pizza.** Hand out paper and pencils; let group members write down what kind of pizza they would like. It is very unlikely that all will be in agreement. After a few minutes, collect the orders and read them aloud. Ask: **Do you think we could come to some agreement on what to order, or should we just forget about it?** See if kids compromise on their initial requests. While waiting for the pizza to arrive, discuss how churches have to make similar decisions—come to agreement or forget about trying to compromise and go their separate ways.

Step 4
Again, you will probably want to work as a single group rather than smaller groups as you discuss the Ephesians passage. As you read the passage aloud, instruct half of your group members to listen for action verbs; instruct the other half to listen for passive ones. Try to do whatever it takes to keep everyone involved and to keep group members interacting with one another. When someone asks a question, see what others in the group think before you jump in with the answer. Try to help kids get excited about the opportunity to work together as a small group to better understand Scripture—and each other.

Large Group

Step 1
Pass out paper and pencils to your group members. Explain to them that you are going to call out various categories of consumer products. When group members hear the category, they are to write down the names of what they think are the top 3 selling brands (in that order—1st, 2nd, 3rd) of that type of product. Some examples of products you might ask are: soda pop, jeans, cars bought in the United States, cereals, athletic shoes, toothpaste, etc. (Note: This is information you will have to obtain.) Afterward, state the correct answers as group members "grade" each other's papers. Award some prize to the person who had the most correct. Then make the point that just like all the different brands of products on the market today had to come from a few original products, church denominations are the same way. There were a few big original denominations that all other denominations have evolved from. Then say that those three—Catholic, Orthodox, and Protestant—are what you are going to take a look at and study today.

Step 3
Have kids form teams of three or four. Hand out paper and pencils. Announce that the teams will be competing to see which can be the first to write down ninety-five different complaints about school. Explain that the complaints may be as specific as "My desk in history class has ten pieces of gum stuck to the bottom of it" or as general as "The teachers are mean." See how long it takes for kids to come up with ninety-five complaints. Award prizes to the winning team. Use this activity to introduce the topic of Martin Luther's ninety-five complaints concerning the Catholic Church.

43

OPTIONS

SESSION TWO

Heard It All Before

Step 1
At the end of Step 1, give your kids an opportunity to show what they know concerning the three major divisions of Christian groups. Ask: **How many of you have ever attended an Orthodox worship service? How many of you have ever attended a Catholic service? How many of you have ever attended a Protestant service? What are some of the differences between the three styles of worship?** Encourage several kids to offer their opinions as to the pros and cons of each style; then ask them to tell you which style they prefer and explain why.

Step 2
Have kids form groups. Instruct each group to come up with a scenario that explains how and why the splits occurred that eventually resulted in the formation of the Orthodox, Catholic, and Protestant churches of today. Encourage the groups to be as outrageous and humorous (without being offensive) as possible in their scenarios—the crazier the explanations, the better. After a few minutes, have each group share its scenario. Afterward, vote as a group on the best one. Lead in to a discussion of the actual reasons for the divisions.

Little Bible Background

Step 2
Kids with little Bible background may perceive "the church" as being something that some people go to and others don't. Depending on kids' previous experience, you will probably want to condense the information in this step. The differences between the Orthodox church and the Roman Catholic church may not be as pressing to your group members as the differences between church people who put fish insignia on their cars and those who don't. You want your group members to know church history, but at this point you need to keep it balanced with what's happening *now*. Until young people understand the current situation, church history isn't likely to matter a lot to them.

Step 3
This step also contains a lot of material that you might want to condense. Perhaps the discussion about Martin Luther will raise questions about other "church people" your group members have heard of, but don't know much about. Be sure to look ahead to the next session to see who will be introduced later, but be ready to answer questions about other people who aren't included in this series. Ideally, the questions at this point will concern the differences between Catholicism and Protestantism, but your group members may not know enough to keep their questions to that narrow a focus. Also use this time to help your group members be completely clear on the salvation-by-faith concept. It's more important for them to understand this essential doctrine than to know about selling indulgences.

Fellowship & Worship

Step 1
Have kids form teams. Instruct the members of each team to plan a trip for their spring break. Emphasize that they need to cover *all* of the details of the trip—from deciding on a destination to choosing where they'll stay to determining how they'll take care of meals. After a few minutes, have each group share its plans. Then ask members from each group to talk about their experiences in making decisions regarding the trip. Ask: **How easy or difficult was this process? What areas were the most difficult to work out? Did people have strong opinions or did they not really care?** At the end of the discussion, point out that planning even a one-week trip can cause disagreements between people. Imagine what can happen between people when the destination is heaven, and the "visit" is for eternity!

Step 4
Write "Mercy is not getting what we deserve; grace is getting what we don't deserve" on the board. Briefly discuss the statement as a group to make sure that your kids understand it. Hand out paper and pencils. Instruct kids to make two columns on their sheet, labeling one column "Grace" and the other column "Mercy." Give group members a few minutes to fill in their columns with examples of grace and mercy that they've seen in their lives. After a few minutes, ask volunteers to share some of the things that they wrote. Close the session by having kids sing or listen to a recording of "Amazing Grace."

OPTIONS

S E S S I O N   T W O

Step 1
When you set up your "pizza parlor," rather than arranging tables, set up stations at which your group members can make real pizzas. Provide each group with all of the necessary ingredients for making a pizza—including an array of possible toppings. Give the groups the same instructions that are in the session plan. When the pizzas are finished, pop them in the oven so that they'll be ready to munch on at the end of the session.

Step 3
As you prepare for the skit on Repro Resource 4, you may wish to invite a male from your church to portray Martin Luther. A rather fun option, however, would be to provide a monk costume for one of your girls and let her play the part. If you get any complaints about playing a guy's role, point out that in Shakespeare's day women weren't allowed to act; men played all of the roles—male and female—in a performance. Turnabout is fair play!

Step 3
Hand out paper and pencils. After you discuss the boldness of Martin Luther, ask your guys to write out a list of things that they would like to see changed about your church. When they finish, they should nail (or tack) their lists to a nearby bulletin board. Since the category is so general, you may get a wide variety of ideas in many areas—what to study, new facilities to build, things to eliminate, and so forth. Encourage your guys to be outspoken about what they believe. Even though they will need to learn to work with other people in order to accomplish their desires, explain that strong feelings are a good start for establishing and maintaining commitment in the church.

Step 4
Begin this step by having guys describe something they have built that they are pretty proud of. This can be anything from a ship in a bottle to a solar system science project to a really delicious submarine sandwich. Try to get your guys to identify with the satisfaction of their *workmanship*. Then, when they get to the discussion of Ephesians 2:10 and discover that they are God's workmanship, perhaps they will relate more strongly to His pride in having created them. Consequently, they should be more willing to place their confidence in Him rather than trying to work out their own salvation, which is sometimes a "guy" attitude toward Christianity.

Step 1
A variation of the opening activity is to let group members create their own pizzas. You should provide the individual crusts and a variety of ingredients, but then let each person assemble his or her own. Don't bring up the theme of the session until everyone is finished. As the pizzas are cooking, have kids describe what they put on their pizzas. See if any two are alike. Then use your kids' natural propensity for variety to explain why there is such a variety of different churches today. Point out that while some things remain the same in essentially all pizzas (crust, cheese, etc.) and churches, the choice of "toppings" can create a vast number of combinations.

Step 4
If you open with the variety-of-pizzas approach to church, conclude with a unity-of-dessert example. Have a dessert item prepared that you know all of your group members enjoy. Challenge kids to remember that in spite of the fact that churches come in all varieties, the members of each church need to strive for unity. Sometimes we must sacrifice personal preference for the good of the group as a whole. So while some of the people may have preferred banana splits, they might have to "settle" in this case for chocolate chip cookies. Thank them for their sacrificial attitudes in this case (and, it is hoped, in more serious instances in the future).

OPTIONS

SESSION TWO

MEDIA

Step 1
Begin the session by playing several brief snippets of songs by Christian artists. Try to include as many different styles of music (rap, pop, country, easy listening, heavy metal, soul, blues, etc.) as possible. After you've played several song clips, have kids vote on which song (or music style) they'd like to hear more of. Ideally, you should get a variety of responses. Then ask: **If we divided up our group according to the music styles that we prefer, how many different groups would we have?** Use the idea of dividing the group according to differing personal tastes and styles to introduce the divisions that occurred in the early church.

Step 3
Expand the "trinket" idea at the beginning of Step 3. Have kids form groups. Give each group one of the trinkets suggested in the text. Instruct the group to create a sales presentation for its item to present on the "Church Shopping Network." The presentation should be as exaggerated and humorous (without being offensive) as possible. After a few minutes, set up your "Church Shopping Network" camera and record each group's presentation. Afterward, play back the tape for your kids to enjoy. Use this activity to introduce the "trinket selling" and other practices of the Roman Catholic Church that Martin Luther objected to.

SHORT MEETING TIME

Step 1
For a shorter opener, try a game of "What's the Difference?" Explain that you'll call out two items; after you do, the first person to stand and name three differences between the two items gets a point. The person with the most points at the end of the game is the winner. Among the pairs of items you might use are crocodile/alligator, Mississippi/Alabama, and dictionary/thesaurus. Use this activity to lead in to a discussion of the differences between Orthodox, Catholic, and Protestant beliefs.

Step 4
Writing questions on the board and having kids form groups to answer them may take longer than you have time for at the end of your session. Instead, simply read aloud Ephesians 2:1-10. Then ask: **What does this passage tell us about good works?** (We are saved by the grace of God, and not by the works that we do. However, we are God's "good work." God has created us to be good. Having received His grace, we can begin to live as He intended all along.) Close the session in prayer, thanking God for His grace and asking Him for the power to live rightly.

URBAN

Step 1
Have kids form groups. Give each group $1,000 in play money. Explain that the money has been earmarked to help inner-city youth. Each group's assignment is to determine exactly how the money should be put to use. For instance, should it be used to help renovate an abandoned building to use as a youth center? Should it be used for drug-awareness education? Should it be used to fund an after-school program? Do *not* appoint a leader for each group. See what happens as the members of each group try to reach a consensus on how to spend the money. After a few minutes, have each group share its plan. Then ask members from each group to talk about their decision-making process. Use this activity to introduce the idea that methods of decision making (or leadership styles) distinguish certain denominations from each other.

Step 3
To begin this step, ask: **Do you think church services in the suburbs or in rural areas are different from church services in the city? If so, how are they different?** Encourage several group members to offer their opinions. Then ask: **Why do you think these differences exist?** Lead in to a discussion of the history of Christianity, focusing specifically on the differences that led to various splits in the church.

OPTIONS

SESSION TWO

Step 2
To help kids see that people are different even when they live in the same general area, divide the group into smaller groups according to the schools they attend. If this will not give you a good balance (or if all of your kids go to one school), divide the group evenly; then assign the members of each small group a school in their area with which they would be familiar. However you divide the group, make sure that junior highers and high schoolers are on separate teams. Hand out paper and pencil. Instruct the members of each group to list as many distinctives as they can think of about their school in the following areas: clothing, slang, sports, clubs, and academics. After groups have assembled their lists, discuss differences and similarities. Then talk about some of the reasons for these differences (age of students, economics of the surrounding neighborhoods, fads that catch on because of unique circumstances, and so on) Point out that there are many factors that influence people's behavior, whether you're talking about school or church.

Step 3
When group members hear about the Reformation, they may be thinking, *So what? We all have complaints about the church.* Bring up this possibility. Then have kids form small groups, making sure that you have an even mix of junior and senior highers in each group. Hand out paper and pencils. Instruct the members of each group to come up with their own list of grievances about the church. However, each grievance must have some kind of biblical support. After a few minutes, have each group share and explain its list. Discuss as a group the grievances on each list. [NOTE: This activity is not designed to give kids a forum for ragging about their church. Instead, it's designed to help them see that often what people complain about are things that are not at all essential to our faith and salvation.]

Step 2
Bring in several books on church history and several books that address the beliefs of Orthodox, Catholic, and Protestant churches. Have kids form three groups. Give each group a stack of books and assign it one of the three major church categories. Instruct the group to find out all it can in 15-20 minutes about the history of its assigned church and the key beliefs that separate its church from the other two. When time is up, have each group present its findings. Discuss any findings that seem to contradict the findings of another group. Use the material in Steps 2 and 3 to supplement and clarify the information provided by the groups.

Step 3
After discussing the practices of the Catholic Church that caused Martin Luther to protest, ask your group members to consider whether there are any practices in Christianity today—perhaps in an area like Christian broadcasting—that might cause someone to protest. Spend a few minutes discussing why such practices might cause a protest; then move on to Step 4.

Date Used:

Approx. Time

Step 1: Pizza! Pizza! _____
o Extra Action
o Small Group
o Large Group
o Heard It All Before
o Fellowship & Worship
o Mostly Girls
o Extra Fun
o Media
o Short Meeting Time
o Urban
Things needed:

Step 2: As Far As the East Is from the West _____
o Extra Action
o Heard It All Before
o Little Bible Background
o Combined Junior High/High School
o Extra Challenge
Things needed:

Step 3: Nailed to the Door _____
o Large Group
o Little Bible Background
o Mostly Girls
o Mostly Guys
o Media
o Urban
o Combined Junior High/High School
o Extra Challenge
Things needed:

Step 4: Saved by Grace _____
o Small Group
o Fellowship & Worship
o Mostly Guys
o Extra Fun
o Short Meeting Time
Things needed:

SESSION 3

Who's Protesting What?

(An Overview of Major Protestant Denominations)

YOUR GOALS FOR THIS SESSION:
Choose one or more

☐ To help kids learn the basics of the history and distinctives of major Protestant denominations.

☐ To help kids understand some of the issues of theology and church life that brought these denominations into being.

☐ To help kids determine to live in the love and power of God's Spirit.

☐ Other _____

Your Bible Base:

Ephesians 6:10-13
I Timothy 1:3-7
Revelation 2:1-6

Going Overboard

(Needed: Materials to make signs)

After welcoming group members, say: **Today we'll be focusing on Protestant denominations. How many Protestant denominations can you think of?** Get a list of several denominations.

Can you think of any denominations that believe pretty much the same thing that we in our church or denomination believe? Be prepared to mention some.

So why do we have different denominations if they believe pretty much the same thing? Let kids take a few stabs at the question. If no one mentions it, point out that it comes down to history. Different groups came into being for different reasons at different times.

Ask: **What does the word "Protestant" mean?** (Protesters. Protestants came into being because they protested certain practices of the Catholic Church. Protestant groups have continued protesting, forming new groups along the way. Some of the protests have been rather petty, but others have helped to bring new life to dead churches.)

Invite all of your group members to join in a roleplay. Explain that they will act out a parable concerning lifeboats that may help them understand denominations.

Say: **We're all in a big ship, crossing the ocean. What's the name of the ship?** Select a name for the ship. Have someone write it on poster board and hold it aloft. **Suddenly a storm comes up and we start to take on water. Who's the captain?** Select a captain. **The captain must get everyone bailing water so that the ship can stay afloat.**

But there are some people on board who feel that the ship is doomed. These people feel it's best to abandon ship, that no amount of bailing will help. Who's the leader of this rebel group? Select a leader. **This leader must convince people to abandon ship and climb into a lifeboat.**

Let the rebel leader lobby for the lifeboat while the captain urges people to stay and bail water. Then divide the lifeboat people (make sure there's at least one other besides the rebel leader) from the ship people. Ask the lifeboat people to choose a name for their vessel and write it on poster board.

Then say: **So now there are two vessels on the ocean—the ship and the lifeboat. The ship gets through the storm, but** pretty soon some questions arise. **The captain seems to be a bit wacky now. Some of you think he's going in the wrong direction. Who's the leader of this new rebel group?** Select a leader. **You feel that it's best to take another lifeboat out and set off in the right direction. So you, rebel leader, try to drum up support as you, Captain, try to keep people on board, in your wacky way.**

Once again, divide this new group of protesters from the main ship. Have members of the new group choose a name for their lifeboat and write it on poster board.

Then say: **Meanwhile, back on the first lifeboat, the passengers are having problems. It seems that the people on one side of the boat can't stand people on the other side. Why?** Have the lifeboat passengers choose a reason for the rift—bad breath, loud snoring coming from one side of the ship, or whatever. **So the people on one side of the boat decide to inflate the raft on this lifeboat and set out on their own.**

Divide the people on one side of the boat from the people on the other side. Have the "rafters" choose a new name for their raft and write it on poster board.

Then say: **Now we have four vessels on the high seas. There might be five more lifeboats on the ship, each one with a raft inside, so we could keep splitting up if need be. But what are the differences among these four groups?**

Interview someone from each of the groups. Ask about that person's attitude toward those in the other groups (within the roleplay, of course). How do the two lifeboat groups differ from each other? Actually, they don't differ very much at all. It's simply a matter of when and why they left the boat. Maybe even some of the raft people, after a few days, realize that their disagreement with the lifeboat people was pretty silly. These groups have a lot of similarity, just like many denominations, but the history of their voyage has put them in different boats.

Explain: **Once you set out in a different boat, it's hard to get back together with your old boat. That's true of denominations too. Each denomination develops its own leadership, its own way of doing business, and its own way of worship. Even if the differences are small, it's hard to merge those things with another denomination. There have been a few mergers in recent years. Several Lutheran groups decided to come together. And Northern Presbyterians and Southern Presbyterians, divided by the Civil War, decided to get back together after 120 years of separation. But these have been exceptions to the rule. Once divided, it's hard to reunite. And, as long as you're not fighting with those in the other lifeboats, that may be just fine.**

CUSTOM CURRICULUM

STEP 2

Four-Lane Highway

(Needed: Copies of Repro Resource 5, pencils)

Ask: **Who was Martin Luther? What did he do? Why?** (Luther sparked the Protestant Reformation with his opposition to corruption in the Roman Catholic Church.)

Explain: **Martin Luther was not the only one who was unhappy with what was going on in the Catholic Church. There were many others who were thinking about reform. In fact, we can identify four main streams of the Reformation. Once we understand these, we can better understand the different denominations in our world today.**

Hand out copies of "Streams of the Reformation" (Repro Resource 5) and pencils. Have kids form four groups. Assign each group one of the "streams" on the sheet. Instruct each group to read its assigned section and come up with five key words to describe that "stream." Give the groups a few minutes to work. When everyone is finished, ask each group to share and explain its five key words.

Afterward, point out that Repro Resource 5 deals only with the four historical streams that emerged in the 1500s. These are four "lifeboats," if you will. There have been many "rafts" that have set off from these movements since then.

STEP 3

In God We Crust

(Needed: Copies of Repro Resource 6, copies of Repro Resource 7, pencils)

Ask: **Have you ever done something that was really fun at first, but then got old and boring? If so, what was it?** Be prepared to share an example from your own life. **Why did the activity get old and boring?** (We humans tend to like new things. In this generation especially, things get boring fast.)

51

Explain: **There's something that happens with church movements that's very similar. You might call it the "crusting" of the church. I could take a luscious piece of bread and put it right here, but what would it look like a week from now? A month from now?** (It would get stale, crusty, moldy, and disgusting.) **It might start off as a great nutritious treat, but after a while, it gets all crusted over and worthless. A similar thing can happen with churches and denominations.**

Hand out copies of "Two Later Streams" (Repro Resource 6). Give group members a few minutes to read through the sheet.

Then say: **The Anglican Church had begun partly because the English didn't want the Roman Catholics telling them what to do. But then the Anglicans began ruling England with a heavier fist, and people who dissented with the official church were arrested. That's how the Baptists came into being, in the early 1600s. It was a dissenting group that actually had to flee from England and go to Holland for a while. There they met some Mennonites and were influenced by Anabaptist teachings. To this day, Baptists believe in believer's baptism and the separation of church and state—two hallmarks of Anabaptist theology.**

The Methodist Church came into being late in the 1700s as a renewal movement within the Anglican Church. Though the Anglicans had started with a wave of spiritual energy, by this time, some felt that they were crusting over, getting a bit moldy. Christianity was a matter of regular churchgoing and good theology, but it didn't seem to be changing people's lives very much. In addition, many poor people didn't feel welcome in the church. John Wesley began to teach people a "method" of Christian growth. Wesley emphasized spiritual exercises, particularly meeting with small groups. But a new spiritual fervency swept through England, and the Methodist Church was born.

Interestingly, within the next century, there were times when the Methodist Church seemed to lose its spark, and other movements broke off in attempts to recapture the original spirit. Among these were the Salvation Army, the Wesleyans, the Nazarenes, the Free Methodists, the Church of God in Christ—and, in a way, the Pentecostal movement.

The following skit may illustrate this pattern of encrusting and renewal. Ask for four volunteers to perform a brief skit. Hand out copies of "Crust and Decay" (Repro Resource 7) to the volunteers. Give them a few minutes to read through the script; then have them perform. [NOTE: We are *not* saying that any of the churches in the skit—Anglican, Catholic, or Methodist—are now "dead" or "crusty." As with the lifeboats, some people stay in the ship and keep bailing. All of

these groups have had significant renewal movements that have stayed within the denomination.]

Afterward, ask: **What was the pattern here? How do you think you'd feel if you were in a church that was getting "crusty"? Why?** Get several responses.

Then say: **There's a new issue that has arisen in the twentieth century. Churches have divided along liberal-conservative lines. Thinkers in some of the major Protestant denominations adopted controversial policies regarding the authority of the Bible; the factuality of Jesus' virgin birth, miracles, and resurrection; women's role in church leadership; the power of the church hierarchy; and other social issues. Some conservatives have felt compelled to spin off new denominations that upheld traditional views of these issues.**

Now, many Christians care more about your conservative or liberal stance on the issues than on your denomination. For example, a conservative Presbyterian has more in common with a conservative Methodist than with a liberal Presbyterian.

First Love

(Needed: Bibles)

Ask kids to turn to Revelation 2:1-6. Read the first verse. Then ask: **Who is speaking? To whom is He speaking?** (Jesus is giving His critique of seven different churches. At this point, He's speaking to the church at Ephesus, the same church that Paul wrote Ephesians to, and where Timothy served as pastor for a while.)

What's this business about the stars and lampstands? (The lampstands represent the churches [see Revelation 1:20]. The point is that Jesus is in control.)

Read Revelation 2:2, 3. Ask: **What good things does Jesus say about the church at Ephesus?** (The people have worked hard and persevered, presumably under difficult circumstances. They have rejected "wicked men" and tested those who claimed to be apostles. They seem to be strong defenders of the true faith.)

Ask volunteers to read Ephesians 6:10-13 and I Timothy 1:3-7. Explain that both of these passages were written to this same church in

Ephesus about thirty years earlier.

Afterward, ask: **What feeling do you get from these verses? What were the people supposed to do? From what we just read in Revelation, do you think they were doing this?** (The earlier texts give us a feeling of battle. There would be false teachers who would have to be stopped. It would be hard work defending the true faith. From the Revelation passage, it would seem that the people did good work.)

Read Revelation 2:4. Ask: **What criticism does Jesus have for this church? What does this mean? How important do you think this is?** (The people had "forsaken [their] first love." This could mean [a] the things they loved to do at first they weren't doing anymore; [b] they had a love for Christ at the beginning that they weren't showing anymore; or [c] they weren't loving *each other* the way they had earlier.)

Do you think this could be an "occupational hazard" for people who are fighting to defend the faith? (It's a leading question, but yes. In the I Timothy passage read earlier, it was stated that the goal of opposing false teachers is love. But that's easy to forget.)

Does this help us understand the history of denominations that we've been learning about? If so, how? (It's not an exact correlation, but it's interesting to see how even the members of a biblical congregation start to "lose it." They're doing everything right, but they forget how to love. That initial spark gets lost in the day-to-day grind. We need to keep reminding ourselves of where we started.)

Read Revelation 2:5, 6. Ask: **What does Jesus want this church to do?** (Repent; change its ways; go back to genuine love.)

Do you think it can be done? If so, how? If not, why not? Get several responses.

Explain: **The Nicolaitans were probably a group that compromised with the surrounding culture. They probably engaged in idol worship and various immorality while still considering themselves good Christians. It's interesting that even after calling the church back to love, Christ affirms the need for righteousness. He's not saying, "Just love everybody and everything will be all right." Our love for God results in righteous behavior. But righteousness without love has no point to it** (see I Corinthians 13:1-3).

Ask: **Is there a point in your Christian life that you need to go back to? Have you dropped something important along the way? It can happen to denominations. It can also happen to individuals—like you and me.**

Close the session with a time of silent prayer, giving kids an opportunity to rediscover their "first love."

"THEY'RE NOT LIKE US!"

REPRO RESOURCE 5a

STREAMS OF THE REFORMATION

1. LUTHERAN

At first, Martin Luther didn't intend to start a new church; he was merely trying to open a theological discussion within the Catholic Church. But he was thrown out of the Catholic Church, and he got backing from a number of German leaders to start a new group.

Luther was most concerned about good theology. He didn't have a problem with all of the liturgical practices of the Catholic Church, so the Lutherans kept a number of these. Even today, some elements of Lutheran worship look a lot like Catholic worship. But Lutherans emphasize the basics of Protestant theology—salvation by grace, the authority of the Bible, and the priesthood of the believer.

Fact File

Spark: Luther's nailing his 95 complaints on the door of the church in Wittenburg, Germany, in 1517; Luther's being thrown out of the Catholic Church in 1521

Location: Lutheranism was originally strong in northern Europe, especially Germany and Scandinavia.

Pioneers: Martin Luther and Philip Melanchthon

Church leadership: Elected bishops

Emphases: Theology; justification by faith

Modern movements: Lutheran churches

2. CALVINIST (REFORMED)

What became known as the "Calvinist" movement actually began before Calvin's conversion, with a priest named Ulrich Zwingli. Serving in Zurich, Switzerland, Zwingli simply began to preach the Bible. This "back to the Bible" movement gained many followers, as people began to question Catholic teachings they believed were not based on Scripture. In 1523, the city-state of Zurich broke from Roman Catholic control and officially sided with Zwingli. Later, the French scholar John Calvin got involved with the Reform movement and wrote its most important books.

While Luther was satisfied to keep some Catholic practices that were based on good theology, the Reform movement wanted to strip away everything that was not found in Scripture. Thus, it rejected much of the ornate ceremony and even the great tradition of religious art. Church buildings were simple, and worship was centered on the reading and preaching of God's Word.

Even today, churches in the Presbyterian and Reformed tradition favor simplicity over ceremony.

Fact File

Spark: Zurich's decision to follow Zwingli in 1523; the publication of Calvin's master work The Institutes in 1536

Location: Calvinism was originally strong in south central Europe, especially Switzerland and France, and in Scotland and Holland.

Pioneers: Ulrich Zwingli, John Calvin, and John Knox

Church leadership: Presbyterian, which means "by elders." Calvinists could not find bishops over lesser officials in the Bible, but they found many teachings about elders. Thus, pastors are viewed as "teaching elders" in the church and serve, along with the "ruling elders" in the region, on the council that runs the churches.

Emphases: The sovereignty of God; God's control of everything

Modern movements: Presbyterian churches (in several different denominations); Reformed churches

"THEY'RE NOT LIKE US!"

REPRO RESOURCE 5b

STREAMS OF THE REFORMATION

3. ANGLICAN

An independence movement was brewing in England long before the Reformation broke out on the continent of Europe. On its own island, the English church was always rather insular, even when officially connected to Rome. Bible translators John Wycliffe (about 1380) and William Tyndale (1525) had attempted to put the Bible in the language of the people. They were met with official opposition, but gained popular support. Increasingly, Christians in England were concerned about Rome's excesses. But the official break with the Roman Church occurred under embarrassing circumstances.

King Henry VIII wanted a divorce, and the Pope would not grant it. So Henry appointed a new archbishop of the English church and ordered him to grant the divorce. In 1534, the English Parliament declared that the King of England was head of the English church and was no longer under the Pope's authority.

So was this just an independent Catholic church or did it open the door to a full-fledged Reformation in England? No one was sure. Lutherans and Calvinists tried to gain power in this theological vacuum, and there was still a large group of Catholic loyalists. Power went back and forth for more than a century. Ultimately, the Anglican Church forged a middle option that was sort of Catholic and sort of Reformed.

To this day, Anglican and (in America) Episcopal churches promote the unity of the church. Their ways of worship run the gamut from simple Protestant to ornate Catholic.

Fact File

Spark: England's Act of Supremacy, in which King Henry VIII became leader of the church in 1534 (although substantial reform didn't start until Edward VI came to the throne in 1547)
Location: England and, later, the United States, Canada, and Australia
Pioneers: Thomas Cranmer and Thomas Cromwell
Church leadership: Episcopal, which means "by bishops." The structure seems similar to the Catholic Church, but the power comes more from below—bishops are elected from among the priests. The head bishop, the Archbishop of Canterbury, is not seen as infallible.
Emphases: Church unity and worship
Modern movements: Anglican and Episcopal churches and major "spinoffs," including the Methodists, Congregationalists, and Baptists

4. ANABAPTIST

Anabaptists were the radical alternative of the Reformation. According to them, no one was reforming the church *enough*. Anabaptist means "those who are baptized again," and it comes from its adherents' insistence on believers' baptism as adults. It's not enough to be sprinkled as a baby, they say; you also have to make a conscious decision to follow Christ and seal that with baptism by a person of sufficient age.

Anabaptists also rejected the church-state connection that other Reformers took for granted. The church, they felt, had a spiritual power independent of any political structure. Anabaptists sought to obey Scripture radically—pushing pacifism, voluntary poverty, personal discipleship, and Christian community.

Of course, they were way too radical for most people in those days. They were persecuted by Catholics, Lutherans, and Calvinists alike. As those three groups carved up the political spoils of Europe in the 1600s, the Anabaptists were virtually ignored.

Some found a home in Holland, which tended to accept everyone. There the Mennonites were founded, and they had a major influence on a group of English rebels who later became known as Baptists.

Fact File

Spark: The rejection of the Anabaptist leaders by the Zurich Council in 1525, which brought new coherence to the group of rebels
Location: Scattered throughout central Europe and, later, Holland
Pioneers: Michael Sattler and Menno Simons
Church leadership: Congregational. Each believer has authority and is accountable to God. Christians may elect leaders, but official hierarchies are avoided.
Emphases: Individual commitment of faith; separation of church and state; authority from Scripture alone
Modern movements: Mennonites (who strongly influenced the early Baptists), Brethren, and Moravians

"THEY'RE NOT LIKE US!" REPRO RESOURCE 6

TWO LATER STREAMS

There are many denominations that flowed out of the original "streams of the Reformation." Here are two of the most notable.

1. BAPTIST

John Smyth was a courageous young preacher who started an illegal Separatist (non-Anglican) church in England. The congregation was forced to flee to Amsterdam. There, they met with some Mennonites, who shared their Anabaptist theology. Some of the English group decided to join the Mennonites, while others returned to England as the first Baptist church.

Fact File

Spark: Smyth's "re-baptizing" of his congregation in 1608
Location: England and America
Pioneers: John Smyth, Thomas Helwys, and Roger Williams (in America)
Church leadership: Pastors chosen by congregation
Emphases: The Bible; individual response of faith; believer's baptism; separation of church and state
Modern movements: Baptist churches

2. METHODIST

John and Charles Wesley were brothers who were serious about their faith. They were Anglican scholars, preachers, and even missionaries, trying hard to earn favor with God. But then each of these brothers had an eye-opening experience of God's grace. They accepted God's forgiveness and assurance in Jesus Christ and began preaching that Good News wherever they could.

The prim and proper Anglicans weren't sure what to make of the spiritual energy of the Wesleys. When the churches closed their doors to them, the Wesleys and George Whitefield would preach in the streets and fields of England. The common people responded in droves.

The Wesleys really weren't trying to start a new denomination, but the Anglican Church was not welcoming this renewal movement. So eventually the Methodists organized as a distinct church.

Fact File

Spark: The Wesleys' conversion, three days apart, in 1738
Location: England and America
Pioneers: John and Charles Wesley; Francis Asbury (in America)
Church leadership: Elected bishops
Emphases: Personal response of faith; holy living as an outworking of the Spirit's transformation
Modern movements: Methodists and later "spinoffs," including Nazarenes, Wesleyans, the Salvaton Army, the Church of God in Christ, and to some extent, the Assemblies of God

"THEY'RE NOT LIKE US!" REPRO RESOURCE 7

CRUST AND DECAY

(A, B, C, and D stand together.)
ALL: We are the church of Jesus Christ.
A: This is exciting!
B: We are preaching the Good News that anyone can know God through Jesus.
C: He forgives our sins!
D: We are showing His love.
(ALL stop and suddenly look very tired.)
A: But now it's the 1500s. We are the Catholic Church.
B: There's a lot of stuff you have to do in order to really know God.
C: He'll still forgive your sins—for a fee!
D: After all, we have this building program.
A: Wait! Something's wrong here!
B: Yeah! Let's get back to the true Gospel!
C: Let's preach the love and forgiveness of Christ!
(A, B, and C separate from D.)
D: Hey, where are you going?
C: We are the Anglican Church now.
B: We're going to do things right!
A: This is exciting!
(A, B, and C stop and suddenly look very tired again.)
A: But now it's the 1700s. We're the Anglican Church—very proper.
B: Knowing God is good, I guess, as long as you're polite about it.
C: Surely God forgives *our* sins, but we don't commit very many. We're good people, unlike those commoners.
A: Wait! Something's wrong here!
B: Yeah! The true Gospel has to be for everyone, rich and poor alike!
(A and B separate from C.)
C: Hey, where are you going?
B: We are the Methodist Church now. We're going to welcome the common people!
A: This is exciting!
(A and B stop and suddenly look very tired again.)
A: But now it's the late 1800s. We're the Methodist Church *(yawn)* and we're kind of bored.
B: Do you remember where we put the Gospel? It was here a second ago.
A: What does it look like?
B: I forget.
A: Wait! Something's wrong here! Christianity can't be just going through the motions. We have to get busy helping people, to trust Christ to change our lives and theirs. It should be exciting!
(A separates from B.)
B: Hey, where are you going?
A: Now I'm the Salvation Army, or the Wesleyans, or the Assemblies of God. This is exciting! But maybe someday I'll forget why I started too.

OPTIONS

SESSION THREE

EXTRA ACTION

Step 1
Begin the session with a game of dodgeball, using three or four playground balls. Start out playing in the traditional way, with two teams throwing balls at each other from behind a line in the middle of the room. When a person is hit by a ball, he or she is out. The first team to eliminate all opposing players is the winner. After the first game, divide each team in half and play a second game using four teams (with the room divided into four sections). Continue dividing the teams until, for the last game, it's every person for himself or herself. Use this activity to introduce your discussion of the splits that have occurred among Protestant denominations.

Step 3
Have kids take turns creating structures out of dominoes or building blocks and then knocking the structures over. Continue the exercise long enough for every person to have several turns. See how long it takes for the "newness" of the activity to wear off and for kids to get bored and start looking for alternatives to the activity. Use this exercise to lead in to the skit on Repro Resource 7.

SMALL GROUP

Step 1
The thought of churches breaking apart and people going separate ways can be a bit scary for a group that is already small. After the lifeboat exercise, ask: **How would you determine whether to compromise what you believe and try to stay "with the boat" or stick by what you believe—even if that means "sailing on your own" for a while?** Have kids consider whether or not the following issues would be important enough to cause them to leave the church and go elsewhere.
• **The board decrees that girls must wear dresses and guys must wear coats and ties to all church meetings.**
• **You can no longer meet in your usual area. You must meet in homes instead.**
• **The church stops believing that Jesus was born of a virgin and rose from the dead.**
• **You wanted the new carpet to be red, but the majority voted for blue.**
• **The pastor leaves and is replaced with a much older man.**

Step 2
The Repro Resource 5 assignment will need to be assigned to individuals or pairs rather than to groups. This might be a bit awkward for some kids because the material tends to be a bit weighty, with unfamiliar names and words and new information. Before you hand out the sheets, give kids a few words of encouragement and challenge them to do the best they can at picking out five key words. Explain that you'll answer everyone's questions as you go along. Then provide plenty of time for your slower readers to soak in all they can and assimilate the information to the best of their ability.

LARGE GROUP

Step 1
With a large group, you might want to use a real-life example instead of the lifeboat exercise. Instruct your group members to begin planning some kind of event. As kids begin to discuss the details of the event, it's likely that there will be some disagreements. If so, have kids divide into groups based on the sides they take during the disagreements. For example, you might ask: **Should we plan a retreat, a fundraiser, or an outreach event?** Kids will then form three groups based on which format they choose. After kids have formed their new groups, you might ask: **Should we be responsible for the food that's served at the event or should the event be catered?** Instruct kids to divide into even smaller groups based on their responses. Continue asking questions to divide the groups until only two or three people remain in each one. Then introduce the topic of denominations, adapting the last paragraph in Step 1.

Step 2
Rather than simply having groups look for five key words in their assigned material, instruct them to come up with a creative way to present the information in their section to the rest of the groups. For example, one group might use a skit to present its information. Another group might create a song. Encourage the groups to be creative in their presentations. After a few minutes, let each group make its presentation.

OPTIONS

SESSION THREE

HEARD IT ALL BEFORE

LITTLE BIBLE BACKGROUND

FELLOWSHIP & WORSHIP

Heard It All Before

Step 2
If your kids are familiar with the details of the Protestant Reformation, try to put a modern spin on the material. Ask: **Are there any issues in the church today that could cause a major split like the one that Martin Luther instigated? If so, what are those issues? If not, why do you suppose that is?** Encourage several group members to offer their opinions.

Step 4
Kids who've been taught about the differences between certain Protestant denominations may never have had a chance to interact with people of different denominations. If this is the case with your group members, plan some kind of activity that can include youth groups from several other churches (of different denominations) in your area. As you plan the activity, encourage your kids to get to know the members of other groups, to discuss not only the differences between their denominations, but the similarities as well.

Little Bible Background

Step 1
To begin the session, ask: **Do you trust what I teach you at these sessions? If so, why? If you doubted some of the things I say, what would you do about it?** Give kids some time to consider this. Some might not yet think to question anything a church teacher would tell them. Some might have had questions, but were not comfortable enough to bring them up. Others might even be uncomfortable at the suggestion that someone might mislead them in their spiritual blindness. If your kids are new to the Bible and want to learn more, they essentially need to trust someone to help them learn and grow spiritually. But they should begin to see eventually that the Bible itself should be their authority more than any human teacher. Explain that many of the groups you will be discussing today were in a similar situation—looking for spiritual truth and trusting their religious leaders. Some of them were eventually misled and had to seek truth and freedom of religion in new settings.

Step 4
When you get to the Bible study, begin with Ephesians 6:10-13 and 1 Timothy 1:3-7. Explain that these passages were written in regard to the church at Ephesus. Have kids suppose that they were in a church that received these letters from a pastor who had been away for a while. How would they feel? How would they respond to the challenges laid out for them? After discussing this, introduce the passage from Revelation. If kids new to Scripture become sidetracked by the prophetic tone and supernatural message from Jesus to John, they will already have discussed the other passages. Kids will also be better able to see that the church in Ephesus started out strong, but gradually lost sight of its "first love."

Fellowship & Worship

Step 1
When kids arrive, have some lively music playing, some food spread out, and some balloons and streamers (or other decorations) adorning the room. In short, get ready for a party! After kids have mingled for a while, stop the music and instruct them to split into groups according to the school they attend, the color of their hair, or some another arbitrary factor that won't cause too many groups to form. Ask the members of each group to talk about the fact that their differences didn't prevent them at all from enjoying the party. In fact, when they weren't focused on their differences, they probably didn't even notice them. Explain: **When we all get to heaven, that's just how it will be. The differences that we see between our denomination and other denominations will disappear. It's good to understand others and their beliefs while we're here on earth, but when we get to heaven, those differences will all be gone.**

Step 4
Challenge your kids to think back over the past few years of their lives to identify what point they need to return to. Hand out paper and writing utensils (colored markers would probably work best). Instruct group members to make a map of their faith, identifying the point they've left, the obstacles along the way that led them astray, and the road they need to take to return. (For example, let's say a person who never had a problem previously with gossip started hanging out with a crowd that gossiped a lot, causing the person to begin to gossip. That person might need to either change friends or learn to tame his or her tongue to not gossip any longer.) After kids have completed their maps, spend some time thanking God for His spiritual guidance—for being our compass—and praising Him for His love for us.

OPTIONS

SESSION THREE

Step 3
Say: **We've been looking at many different churches, started by many different men. Have you ever wondered what a movement founded by women might be like?** Refer group members back to Repro Resources 5 and 6, instructing them to focus on the distinctives of each group. Then, in groups of three or four, have them put together their "own" movement, based on Scripture and what *they* feel is important. After a few minutes, ask each group to share what it came up with.

Step 4
Say: **We've talked a lot about some strong men of faith; now let's look at some women. Bring in resource materials on women** such as Catherine Booth, Joan of Arc, Catherine Marshall, Saint Margaret of Scotland, Saint Bridget of Sweden, Saint Clare of Assisi, or any other women that you may admire. Allow your girls time to peruse the material and discuss things about these women that they admire. There are many examples of strong women of faith throughout history. Your girls deserve to know them!

Step 2
Since the church has had such a male-dominated history, let your guys present the material from Repro Resource 5 in the roles of the men who were responsible. Some guys may portray the church founders (Luther, Zwingli, Calvin, Wycliff and Tyndale, the two Wesleys, and so forth). Others may portray historical figures who were partially responsible (popes, King Henry VIII, or whomever). As much as possible, have guys make their reports in first person, with comments as appropriate from "supporting characters."

Step 3
Explain during this step that you've been looking exclusively at churches, but that's only part of the potential problem. Yes, if a church isn't careful, it can get "crusty" and lose its "fresh" influence for God on a community. That's the part of the problem this series has dealt with so far. But another problem to be considered is whether the church members truly give the church an opportunity to be influential. Sometimes it's the *people* who get crusty and leave the church without ever giving it a fair chance. Ask: **If your current spiritual life were represented by a piece of bread, would it be (a) a fresh, hot home-made roll right out of the oven; (b) a piece of bread from the center of a loaf, an entire week prior to its expiration date; (c) the end piece of a loaf from the day-old shelf; or (d) a crouton?** After your guys answer, ask: **What other foods would you compare yourself to, in a spiritual sense? Why?**

Step 2
If you think your kids can handle it, try to have them write funny skits that symbolize the conflicts of the people described on Repro Resource 5 rather than approaching them purely from a historical context. For example, Martin Luther's opposition to the existing leaders of the Catholic church could be presented as a well-thought-out verbal presentation. Or it could be acted out as a World Federation Wrestling Match, an encounter on "American Gladiators," a confrontation with pirates in which Luther is forced to "walk the plank," an arm-wrestling challenge, or any number of things. After kids have fun with their presentations, you can quickly summarize the historical truth of the skits that have been acted out.

Step 3
Have several volunteers agree to set up churches of their own and try to sway the rest of the group members to leave your church to join theirs. One person might have a refreshment-oriented church where every service includes doughnuts. Another person might have a "singles" church where guys and girls go to church together—and frequently out to lunch together afterward. Another person might have a church of leisure—with no services longer than fifteen minutes and little, if any, commitment required. Give your volunteers some ideas or see what they can come up with on their own. Then see if they can persuade the other group members to "come on over" to their church. Afterward, make it clear that the Reformation wasn't the result of such petty and cosmetic changes in church function, but was due to significant theological differences.

OPTIONS

SESSION THREE

Step 1
To begin the session, play some scenes (which you've prescreened) from recent video releases that feature characters attending and worshiping in a Protestant church. If you can't find any recent releases that fit the bill, try using an older movie like *Footloose*. Compare the portrayals of Protestant worship services in the movies to the worship service of your own church. How are they similar? How are they different?

Step 2
Before the session, you'll need to record some clips (perhaps from TV newscasts) of various types of protests. If possible, try to show some peaceful protests as well as some protests that turned violent. Show the clips to your group members. Then ask your group members what they think the various protests against the Roman Catholic church (by Martin Luther, Ulrich Zwingli, and others) were like. Lead in to a discussion of the various Protestant denominations that were formed as a result of those protests.

Step 1
Rather than going through the time-consuming lifeboat exercise, try a shorter, simpler method for splitting up your group members. For example, you might have kids form four groups based on the following criteria: kids who have no siblings, kids with one sibling, kids with two siblings, and kids with two or more siblings. After kids have formed groups accordingly, you might divide them further by using categories such as kids who are satisfied with the size of their family and kids who wish their family was a different size. At that point, each group would then split into subgroups. Continue dividing the groups until only one or two people remain in each one. Then introduce the topic of denominations, adapting the last paragraph in Step 1.

Step 2
Combine Steps 2 and 3 by presenting Repro Resources 5 and 6 at the same time. Summarize the information in each section in one or two sentences. (For example, to summarize the "Lutheran" section, you might say: **After splitting from the Catholic church, Luther kept a number of the church's liturgical practices. And while some elements of Lutheran worship today look a lot like Catholic worship, Lutherans emphasize the basics of Protestant theology.**) Skip the "Fact File" sections, except perhaps to mention the "modern movements" of each group. Briefly go through the information in the session regarding the Anglican church and the Methodist church. Skip Repro Resource 7 and move directly to Step 4.

Step 2
To begin this step, ask group members to name as many things as they can think of that people protest. Kids may name things like abortion, job conditions, court rulings, government actions, and so forth. Briefly discuss as a group some of the different forms that protest takes (boycotts, letter-writing campaigns, picket lines, and so on). Then ask: **Have you ever felt so strongly about something that you protested? If so, what was it? Why did you feel so strongly about it?** Lead in to a discussion of the protests against the Roman Catholic church that led to the Protestant Reformation.

Step 4
Invite representatives from one or more Protestant denominations to your meeting. Ask each representative to talk about some of things his or her denomination is doing in the inner city. Perhaps each representative might discuss some of the programs his or her denomination runs for the homeless and needy, some of the organizations the denomination sponsors, and so on. Also encourage each representative to share some information on what your group members can do if they're interested in getting involved in one or more of the denomination's programs.

OPTIONS

S E S S I O N   T H R E E

Step 2
Repro Resource 5 may be a bit difficult for your junior highers. You may wish to pair them with high schoolers as you're dividing into groups to work on the sheet. Or you may want to make a chart of the information on Repro Resource 5 and place it where all can see it easily. Then you could work through Repro Resource 5 together, discussing the information as a group.

Step 4
Many adults have difficulty understanding the Book of Revelation, so this step may be a real challenge for your junior highers. Prior to your meeting, create a poster that displays each of the symbols mentioned and explains what each represents. As you read the verses together, refer to the poster to help your kids discern the message included in the passage.

Step 3
Bring in some kind of chart or diagram that shows the various divisions and formations of Protestant denominations throughout history. Let your group members spend some time discovering which groups split from which organizations and when. If your church belongs to a Protestant denomination, let your kids trace the "family tree" of your denomination. Your group members may be surprised to discover how many different denominations and groups there are within the realm of Protestantism.

Step 4
Bring in several reference books that explain the beliefs of various Protestant denominations—preferably books that contrast and compare the different beliefs. Instruct your group members to create a pamphlet that explains how the beliefs and practices of various denominations differ from the beliefs and practices of your church. If done well, the pamphlet could be used as a resource in your church's library.

Date Used:

Approx. Time

Step 1: Going Overboard _____
o Extra Action
o Small Group
o Large Group
o Little Bible Background
o Fellowship & Worship
o Media
o Short Meeting Time
Things needed:

Step 2: Four-Lane Highway _____
o Small Group
o Large Group
o Heard It All Before
o Mostly Guys
o Extra Fun
o Media
o Short Meeting Time
o Urban
o Combined Junior High/High School
Things needed:

Step 3: In God We Crust _____
o Extra Action
o Mostly Girls
o Mostly Guys
o Extra Fun
o Extra Challenge
Things needed:

Step 4: First Love _____
o Heard It All Before
o Little Bible Background
o Fellowship & Worship
o Mostly Girls
o Urban
o Combined Junior High/High School
o Extra Challenge
Things needed:

SESSION 4

When the Spirit Moves
(What Pentecostals and Charismatics Believe)

YOUR GOALS FOR THIS SESSION:
Choose one or more

☐ To help kids learn the basics of the history and distinctives of Pentecostals and Charismatics.

☐ To help kids understand what the Bible teaches about the Holy Spirit.

☐ To help kids tap into God's power for their own lives.

☐ Other _____

Your Bible Base:

Acts 2:1-4
1 Corinthians 12:4-11; 13:8-13; 14:1-20, 22-33
Galatians 5:22-26

Plan Scan

Have kids form small groups. Ask each group to make plans for a social activity for your youth group or Sunday school class. Give the groups freedom to plan any kind of activity they want. (Of course, that doesn't mean the activity is going to happen.) Emphasize that you're looking for a *plan,* not just an idea. The groups must consider as many details as possible—specifically the arrangements that will need to be made—as they come up with their plans. Give the groups about five minutes to make their plans. When everyone is finished, have each group share its plan.

Afterward, ask: **As you made these plans in your groups, did you find that some people were very detail-oriented, while others wanted to play it by ear?** Ask who was which kind of person. **How did that affect the way you worked together?** Get a couple of responses.

Say: **There are various personality tests that are used to figure out the different ways people think. One of the frequently mentioned differences is that some people seem to play everything by ear, while others need everything decided specifically. One group says things like, "We'll cross that bridge when we get to it." The other group says things like, "If you fail to plan, you plan to fail."**

Ask: **If you had to characterize God and the way He deals with us as one of these two types, which would it be?** Of course, there's no right or wrong answer here. Scripture presents God as decisive and constant, but at the same time flexible and surprising.

Explain: **Today we'll be talking about Pentecostals and Charismatics. We will deal with a number of questions about the Bible and how to interpret it. But there are also personality questions involved. Charismatic worship tends to be more free-flowing—in the *Spirit's* control. If you're a detail-oriented person who likes things well-planned, this kind of worship may be difficult for you. If you're a "play it by ear" kind of person, this type of worship may be right up your alley.** [NOTE: We're not suggesting that all Pentecostals are one way and all non-Pentecostals are another. But the personality questions add to the mix of theological and biblical issues.]

Say: **As we investigate these issues today, let's get past** personality biases. Don't just say "That's weird" or "That's cool." Let's look at what the Bible says about how God works.

STEP 2

How It Started

(Needed: Copies of Repro Resource 8)

Hand out copies of "The Pentecostal and Charismatic Movements" (Repro Resource 8). Give kids a few minutes to read through the sheet.

Have someone read Acts 2:1-4. Then ask: **When the church started on the day of Pentecost, how did the Holy Spirit let people know He was there?** (He gave the apostles the power to speak in tongues.)

To supplement your discussion of Repro Resource 8, use as much or as little of the following information as you desire:

Bible students debate whether Bible texts refer to mysterious empowerment to speak other languages or whether this was some heavenly language that the Spirit allowed the hearers to understand. The result at Pentecost was that people from many nations understood what was said—three thousand of whom became Christians that day.

Throughout the Book of Acts, there are several more occasions when newly converted people were filled with God's Spirit and spoke in tongues.

At various times throughout church history, there were reports of isolated groups or individuals expressing their worship in "pentecostal" ways—with tongues and sort of a spiritual "moshing."

But the modern Pentecostal movement erupted in Los Angeles in 1906. Revival meetings were held at a beat-up old church building on Azusa Street. People were not only getting saved and sanctified, they were speaking in tongues. Soon similar meetings were being held around the country and around the world. Within the next decade or two, several institutions and denominations were formed to promote this "Pentecostal" faith. Among these were the Assemblies of God, which is now the largest Pentecostal denomination.

Pentecostals believe the full Christian experience can only come through the baptism of the Spirit. This, they teach, is a second experience, after salvation. According to most Pentecostal groups, the baptism of the Spirit is almost always accompanied by tongues-speaking.

Pentecostals are also noted for their belief in other gifts of the Spirit such as prophecy and healing. Their worship services are filled not only with tongues-speaking, but also with other phenomena such as "singing in the Spirit" and being "slain in the Spirit."

In many other respects, Pentecostals tend to be like other fundamentalist Protestants. They believe the Bible and tend to take it quite literally. And they emphasize the importance of personal holiness, sometimes observing strict codes of conduct.

A second wave occurred in the 1960s. This became known as the Charismatic Movement, and it grew out of non-Pentecostal churches. Suddenly there were pockets of people in Episcopal, Lutheran, and even Catholic churches who were being "baptized in the Spirit" and speaking in tongues. In some cases, entire churches "went Charismatic." Some churches split over the issue. And in many non-Charismatic churches, there are small Charismatic groups that meet regularly for worship and sharing. There are also some new Charismatic churches that have been started in the last thirty years or so.

For the most part, these Charismatic groups are not tied in with the traditional Pentecostal churches, even though their theology is similar. The Charismatic Movement has been known for its new style of worship—guitars, choruses, informal sharing, hand-raising—which is probably a throwback to the decade when it started, the 1960s. But many non-Charismatic churches have also adopted this style of worship, without accepting the teaching about modern tongues-speaking or other spectacular spiritual gifts.

STEP 3

Back to the Bible

(Needed: Bibles, copies of Repro Resource 9, pencils)

Say: **Let's look at some of the key Bible texts about spiritual gifts and speaking in tongues.**

Have kids form four groups. Hand out copies of "Spirit Search" (Repro Resource 9) and pencils. Assign the following passages:

Group 1—I Corinthians 12:4-11
Group 2—I Corinthians 13:8-13
Group 3—I Corinthians 14:1-20
Group 4—I Corinthians 14:22-33

Give the groups a few minutes to read their assigned passages and answer the questions on the sheet. When everyone is finished, have each group share its responses. Use the following information to supplement the groups' responses, as needed.

Group 1—1 Corinthians 12:4-11
What would you say is the main point of this passage? (The unity of the church amid the diversity of spiritual gifts.)
Why are spiritual gifts—the "manifestation of the Spirit" (12:7)—given? ("For the common good"—that is, not for anyone's individual pleasure or privilege.)
Have you ever seen a Christian use any of the gifts mentioned here? If so, how were the gifts used? Be prepared to share some examples that you've seen.
How would you define "the message of wisdom" (12:8)? "The message of knowledge" (12:8)? "Distinguishing between spirits" (12:10)? (Non-Pentecostals are likely to define "the message of wisdom" as good leadership, "the message of knowledge" as good teaching, and "distinguishing between spirits" as keen perception about people's motives. The Pentecostal interpretations of those gifts are more spectacular, involving God's giving specific messages to the church through gifted individuals.)

Group 2—1 Corinthians 13:8-13
What would you say is the main point of this passage? (Love is the most important thing for a Christian.)
What things will "cease," "be stilled," or "pass away" (13:8)? What do you think this means? (Prophecies, tongues, and knowledge. Compared to love, these are all temporary. Our experience of knowing and expressing God is partial now, but love draws us into the eternal heart of God.)
What do you think "childish ways" (13:11) might include? (In context, all three gifts—prophecy, tongues, and knowledge—would have to be included. It could be that the Corinthians were childishly fighting over the gifts, and that Paul was chastising them by reminding them that all gifts are childish compared to love.)
Some non-Pentecostals say that this passage refers to the stopping of the "supernatural" gifts, such as speaking in tongues. These gifts, they say, were intended as signs for the early church that God was at work, but that the church would eventually outgrow its need for these ifts. Do you agree or disagree with this theory? Why? Be prepared to share your church's beliefs on this matter here.

Group 3—1 Corinthians 14:1-20
What would you say is the main point of this passage? (Prophecy is a more helpful gift than speaking in tongues. It is preferable to be understood.)
What gift does the author, Paul, seem to prefer over speaking in tongues? Why? (Prophecy, because all can understand it.)

What does Paul say about his own personal devotions (14:18)? (He spoke in tongues frequently in private, but not in the church.)

In what way do you think the Corinthians were "thinking like children" (14:20)? (Perhaps in their bickering over their spiritual gifts. Perhaps in desiring the more spectacular gifts.)

Group 4—I Corinthians 14:22-33
What would you say is the main point of this passage? (Worship should be both orderly and intelligible to the outsider.)

What does the author, Paul, say about the purpose of speaking in tongues? (It's a sign for unbelievers—possibly to say, "Hey! Something really cool is going on here! Pay attention!")

What instructions does Paul give for speaking in tongues in church? (Only two or three should speak in a meeting—one at a time. There must be an interpreter. It should be orderly.)

What does Paul mean by "the spirits of prophets are subject to the control of prophets" (14:32)? (Those who proclaim God's truth are not out of control. They should not enter into some ecstatic frenzy as some pagan prophets did.)

Voices

(Needed: Copies of Repro Resource 10)

Hand out copies of "Voices in the Wind" (Repro Resource 10). Explain that these statements reflect the way some young people might feel about Pentecostal or Charismatic groups. Go through the statements one at a time. After you read each one, ask: **What would you say to this person? Do you think this person is reacting well? What cautions or corrections would you suggest to the person regarding her reaction?**

Use the following information to supplement your discussion of Repro Resource 10. (Your responses will, of course, depend on your church's attitude toward the charismatic gifts, the baptism of the Holy Spirit, and speaking in tongues.)

Marty seems to be reacting to the external appearance of charismatic worship. She needs to get past the "weirdness" and really deal with the underlying beliefs.

Michelle obviously had some stagnation in her Christian life. For

Charismatics, this is a classic case of someone in need of Spirit baptism. Non-Charismatics might see this as a spiritual reawakening, an energizing—even a "filling" with the Spirit—but not the first-time entry of the Spirit. Can we affirm Michelle's new commitment, even if we don't agree with the Charismatic interpretation of what happened to her?

Tara is having the problem that many non-Charismatics have with Charismatics. It's the promise of a higher level. This is the central theological difference between the two camps. Is there a second blessing required? Does the Spirit enter the believer at a point beyond salvation, or is it all a "package deal"?

As you close the session, read Galatians 5:22-26. Encourage your group members to "keep in step with the Spirit" in their daily lives.

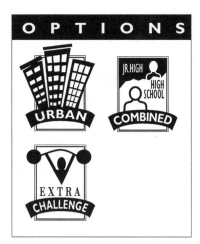

"THEY'RE NOT LIKE US!"

REPRO RESOURCE 8

The Pentecostal and Charismatic Movements

ORIGINS
Pentecostal: There were some stirrings in late 1800s, but the movement erupted in 1906 in Los Angeles. Revival meetings spread and new denominations were formed.
Charismatic: The movement began in 1960, in an Episcopal Church in Van Nuys, California, and spread through small groups in mainline Protestant and Catholic churches.

KEY BELIEFS
- *Baptism by the Holy Spirit as a second blessing.* Salvation is step one. For the full experience of Christ, one must be filled with the Spirit.
- *Speaking in tongues.* This always accompanies Spirit baptism. It is the evidence that one has received the baptism. (Some Charismatics are less dogmatic than others about the necessity of speaking in tongues.)
- *All spiritual gifts are active today.* While many other Christians believe that "supernatural" gifts such as healing were intended only for the early church, Pentecostals and Charismatics see no reason why these gifts should not be used today.

CHARACTERISTICS
- *Lively worship.* If the Spirit is running the show, who knows what will happen? The Charismatic movement in particular has developed an accessible, energetic worship style.
- *Personal holiness.* If one is filled by the Spirit, his or her life should please the Spirit. The traditional Pentecostal churches especially emphasize the "sanctified" lifestyle and sometimes place strict requirements on behavior.
- *Emotional devotion.* While other Christians may emphasize a mental understanding of God's Word, Pentecostals and Charismatics tend to emphasize the emotional side. Worship services are often highly emotional, as are the individuals' personal worship times.

PRACTICES THAT MAY NEED EXPLANATION
- *Speaking in tongues.* This is considered a heavenly praise language. Sometimes God gives a message to the church through someone speaking in tongues, in which case an interpreter must translate for the congregation.
- *Healing.* Pentecostals and Charismatics still uphold this biblical gift, although they maintain that only certain people possess the gift. "Laying on of hands" is often the way this power is transmitted.
- *Prophecy.* Pentecostals and Charismatics still uphold this biblical gift, which involves relating a message from God concerning future events. Most non-Charismatics who are uneasy about getting new messages from God interpret this gift as preaching, the proclamation of God's Word.
- *The word of knowledge.* A person with this gift can tell another person exactly what's wrong with him or her and exactly what to do, even if the two have never met before. This is another biblical gift that non-Charismatics interpret in a less supernatural way.
- *Singing in the Spirit.* This is a worship activity in which a song starts in the congregation and just flows along, led by the Spirit. People may be singing different tunes and different words, or no words at all, but the intention is Spirit-led praise.
- *Being "slain in the Spirit."* This is a popular practice among traveling preachers and faith healers. A person is "touched" with the power of God and falls back, as if dead. It is seen as a testimony to God's power and perhaps as a kind of baptism—death and new life.

"THEY'RE NOT LIKE US!" REPRO RESOURCE 9

Spirit Search

Group 1—I Corinthians 12:4-11
What would you say is the main point of this passage?

Why are spiritual gifts—the "manifestation of the Spirit" (12:7)—given?

Have you ever seen a Christian use any of the gifts mentioned here? If so, how were the gifts used?

How would you define "the message of wisdom" (12:8)? "The message of knowledge" (12:8)? "Distinguishing between spirits" (12:10)?

Group 2—I Corinthians 13:8-13
What would you say is the main point of this passage?

What things will "cease," "be stilled," or "pass away" (13:8)? What do you think this means?

What do you think "childish ways" (13:11) might include?

Some non-Pentecostals say that this passage refers to the stopping of the "supernatural" gifts, such as speaking in tongues. These gifts, they say, were intended as signs for the early church that God was at work, but that the church would eventually outgrow its need for these gifts. Do you agree or disagree with this theory? Why?

Group 3—I Corinthians 14:1-20
What would you say is the main point of this passage?

What gift does the author, Paul, seem to prefer over speaking in tongues? Why?

What does Paul say about his own personal devotions (14:18)?

In what way do you think the Corinthians were "thinking like children" (14:20)?

Group 4—I Corinthians 14:22-33
What would you say is the main point of this passage?

What does the author, Paul, say about the purpose of speaking in tongues?

What instructions does Paul give for speaking in tongues in church?

What does Paul mean by "the spirits of prophets are subject to the control of prophets" (14:32)?

"THEY'RE NOT LIKE US!"

REPRO RESOURCE 10

Voices in the Wind

Marty
A friend of mine invited me to her church service, but I didn't know what I was getting into. She told me the church was "charismatic," but I honestly thought that just meant the people were really friendly. Everything seemed normal, at first. We sang these choruses for a while, but then it got really weird. This strange kind of song started. Everyone was singing something different. It got louder, and then softer, and then louder again. It was like we were on Mars or something. Then people started standing up and talking gibberish, and everyone was raising his or her hands in the air. Somebody cried out that he'd been healed. Somebody else said that he knew there was someone in the room who had doubts and he looked right at me. I just wanted to get out of there. They say they're Christians, and maybe they are, but I don't see why they can't just worship like normal people.

Michelle
I've been a Christian all of my life—well, since I was six. I tried to live right and all, but it was always kind of dull. You know? Like I was missing something. So then I went on this retreat with some friends. They were Christians, too, but they weren't from my church. They started talking about the Holy Spirit, and it was, like, really obvious that they were talking about something I didn't have. I mean joy and excitement. I always believed in the Holy Spirit, but I didn't know much about Him. So they were all praying for me that I would get baptized in the Spirit, and they told me how I'd just start speaking in tongues and all. And then it happened. It was such an incredible thing. I was blanking out with joy and saying things I didn't understand. But it was really cool. Anyway, now I'm back home and going to my old church. The people here don't believe in speaking in tongues. I'm afraid to tell anyone, because he or she might think I was really wrong. But I just know it's right. You know?

Tara
My cousin goes to a Pentecostal church and she's been spending the summer with my family. She's pretty cool, but all summer she's been ragging me about my faith. I'm a Christian. I was saved three years ago. But she says I need something more. She says I need the Holy Spirit to come upon me or else I'm not a "full" Christian. I really hate it when she says that because it makes me feel like she's holy and I'm not. But do I really need that? I thought the Holy Spirit was inside me *now*. That's what I was always taught. Is there really something else I need? My cousin points out every bad thing I do now and tells me that I need the Spirit. If I was baptized in the Spirit, she says, I wouldn't do those bad things. I don't know what to do.

OPTIONS

SESSION FOUR

Extra Action

Step 1
Try a more active opener. Ask a series of personal-preference questions. For each question, kids will indicate their responses by moving to one side of the room or the other. For example, you might ask: **Would you rather play a sport yourself or watch someone else play it on TV?** Designate one side of the room as "Play it yourself" and the other side as "Watch it on TV." Kids should not only choose which side of the room to move to, but should also indicate the strength of their feelings by standing as close to or as far away from the wall on that side of the room as is appropriate. The closer someone stands to a wall, the more strongly he or she feels about the issue. You might ask questions concerning kids' preference between junk food and gourmet meals, between living in a warm climate and a living in cold climate, and so on. For the final question, ask: **Do you prefer an orderly, restrained worship service or a free-flowing, active service?** After kids respond, move to Step 2.

Step 2
Play a variation of the old TV game show "To Tell the Truth," using Repro Resource 8. Before you distribute copies of the sheet, hand out index cards to six volunteers. Each card should have one of the "Practices That May Need Explanation" written on it, along with the accompanying explanation. Instruct each of your volunteers to come up with two other plausible-sounding explanations for his or her assigned practice. Explain that the volunteers' goal is to trick other group members into believing one of the made-up explanations. After a few minutes, have each volunteer identify his or her practice and then read the three explanations. See how many of your group members can identify the correct explanation. Afterward, hand out copies of Repro Resource 8 and go through the sheet as a group.

Small Group

Step 1
A small group might not have as many different types of people as the average large group, so you may need to adapt the opening activity. Designate one wall of the room as "Totally True" and the opposite wall as "Completely False." Then read a number of statements and have kids stand (literally) where they stand (philosophically) in response to each statement. Here are some statements you might use:
- **I am a spontaneous person. I like things to happen that I don't expect.**
- **If I were told I could go to Florida for a week—all expenses paid—if I could get ready in fifteen minutes, you could count on me to be there in ten.**
- **I know where I want to go to college.**
- **I know what I want to be when I get out of college.**

Use statements that will help your kids show whether they're "play it by ear" people or "I need to have a plan" people.

Step 3
You have a lot of biblical material to cover, so you'll probably need to divide into groups—even though you may have groups of only one or two people. Be careful not to make your small groups responsible for knowing all of the answers to your questions. Many kids feel awkward enough in a group of five or six, much less when they're expected to deal with a difficult passage on their own or in pairs. When you're asking questions, help your kids with their answers. You'll probably be in a hurry to cover so much material, but don't forget to affirm your kids as you go along. Some of what you're assigning is from passages of Scripture that your church may not cover on a regular basis. It might be completely new to your kids, so help them through it as much as you can.

Large Group

Step 1
Begin the session by letting group members sing one of their favorite up-tempo songs or choruses. Sing it through the first time as you normally would. For the second time, incorporate hand clapping and foot stomping. For the third time, let group members create some hand motions or dance steps to accompany the song. Each time group members sing the song, encourage them to be a little more active and raucous. See what happens on about the fifth or sixth time through the song. Afterward, ask your group members whether they prefer a more orderly, restrained style of worship or a more free-flowing, active form of worship. Use the discussion to introduce the material on Repro Resource 8.

Step 3
Rather than simply having groups answer their assigned questions, instruct each group to come up with a creative way to present the information in its passage to the rest of the groups. For example, Group 1 might use a skit to present the information in I Corinthians 12:4-11. Group 2 might create a song or a rap to communicate the information in I Corinthians 13:8-13. Encourage the groups to be imaginative in their presentations. However, emphasize that all of the group's assigned questions must be answered in the course of the presentation. After a few minutes, let each group make its presentation.

OPTIONS

SESSION FOUR

Step 2
If your kids are convinced that they know everything there is to know about Pentecostal and Charismatic beliefs, give them a chance to prove it. Test them on the material on Repro Resource 8. For example, you might ask: **According to Pentecostal belief, what does it mean to be "filled with the Spirit"? What does it mean to be "slain in the Spirit"?** To make things more interesting, you might set up an agreement with your group members before they take the test. You might decide that if they get a certain number of answers right on the test, they will get to choose the closing activity for the session. If, however, they don't get a certain number of answers right, they must spend the last ten minutes of the session cleaning up your meeting area (or doing some other unpleasant task).

Step 4
If your church is non-Pentecostal and non-Charismatic, you may find that some of your kids have preconceived notions about what Pentecostals and Charismatics are like. If so, give your group members an opportunity to rub elbows with kids from a Pentecostal or Charismatic church in your area. Invite your visitors over for an afternoon or evening of fellowship, competition, and discussion. Give your group members (as well as the kids from the visiting church) a chance to discover not only the differences between the two groups, but the similarities as well.

Step 3
If your kids don't know much about Scripture, this would be a very difficult place for them to begin to explore on their own. Consequently, it would probably be better for you to study each passage as a single group—even if you need to reduce the amount of Scripture covered. It will probably be best if *you* read each passage as group members follow along. Then, as you ask the questions, kids can look together for the answers. That way, they can also work together when any of them have questions of their own. Also be sure to tailor the questions to apply more to "first-timers" than to people already comfortable with Scripture and the workings of a church.

Step 4
Of all of the Scripture covered in this session, the closing passage from Galatians 5:22-26 is probably the most important for kids who haven't accumulated a lot of Bible knowledge. Don't skip it or rush through it. After dealing with the working of the Holy Spirit in ways that may seem strange to your kids (especially if your church is not Pentecostal or Charismatic), be sure to let them see the very practical ways that the Holy Spirit equips *all* Christians. Let each person rate the presence of each of the nine spiritual qualities (vss. 22, 23) in his or her life on a scale of one (least) to ten (most). The easiest way to do this is to read one quality at a time and let each person hold up a number of fingers to indicate how well-equipped the person feels in that area. Explain that only by becoming more sensitive to the presence of the Holy Spirit in our lives and keeping in step with Him will we be able to improve the scores we have given ourselves.

Step 1
When the group arrives, have several different flavors of popcorn available throughout the room. As kids mingle, encourage them to choose their favorite flavor. When you're ready to start the session, take a survey of who preferred which flavor. Then ask: **Does the fact that some of you prefer caramel corn while others prefer cheese popcorn change the fact that both groups like popcorn?** (No. They're just variations on the same theme.) **In a similar vein, do you think differences in worship styles really matter as long as the worship goes to God?** You may need to be careful here. Point out that not just any worship is OK; it must be biblically based. There are many ways to interpret Scripture, however; as long as the worship foundation is on target, differences in style probably don't matter much.

Step 4
After reading Galatians 5:22-26, ask: **What does this passage say to you today? What areas of your life does it address?** Hand out paper and pencils. Challenge group members to write a prayer to God, asking His for help in areas of their life that need work and offering praise for areas in their life that are "in step with the Spirit."

OPTIONS

SESSION FOUR

Step 2
Before you begin Step 2, hand out paper and pencils. Ask your girls to write down what they think of when they hear the words "Pentecostal" and "Charismatic." Explain: **Many of us who are not familiar with these worship styles have our own ideas—and sometimes our own misconceptions—of what they are.** Work through Repro Resource 8; then come back to your group members' lists to discuss how accurate their ideas were.

Step 4
Have your group members form pairs. Encourage the members of each pair to share with each other something that they know they need to do this week in order to "keep in step with the Spirit." Allow time for your girls to pray with their partners; then challenge them to pray for each other throughout the rest of the week.

Step 2
Begin this step by letting guys imitate their favorite TV preachers. Many guys, when they see a preacher on TV once or twice, tend to form immediate opinions. They particularly tend to criticize and make fun of things they don't understand. Consequently, guys from non-Charismatic churches may tend to make fun when they see people being "slain in the Spirit" or healed, or when they see other things that aren't done in their own churches. After you witness the performances of your guys, you'll probably be able to tell which preachers (and denominations) kids have been watching. It should also clue you in to any advance prejudices you should deal with during the session.

Step 4
Many times guys are overly critical of church things—especially things that are new to them. But it's surprising to see how accepting they can become as soon as they begin to date girls who attend churches where all of those "strange" things are going on. Adapt the three readings on Repro Resource 10 to represent guys talking about girls they really like and are dating. In the context of trying to maintain a strong relationship with a member of the opposite sex, your guys are likely to become immediately more sensitive and helpful. Their advice will probably be more from the heart in such cases rather than merely from the head.

Step 1
Hand out paper and pencils. Have kids write down a number of questions that begin with the phrase "Would you rather . . . ?" For each question, they should try to think of some very hard decisions for someone to make. For example, they might ask, "Would you rather eat a big piece of liver or get kissed by your great-aunt who always slobbers all over your face?" or "Would you rather go on a date with someone who annoys you half to death or stay home with your parents who annoy you half to death?" After a few minutes, collect the sheets. Then, one at a time, have kids draw a slip and answer the question. If kids come up with some good questions, it will be interesting to watch the reactions of the people who answer. Some are likely to be decisive and sure of themselves in almost every case. Others are likely to waffle back and forth for a while before answering. This activity can replace the planning exercise that opens the session and can lead in to the discussion of the different forms of worship.

Step 2
Let group members write out (or simply tell about) their most unusual or embarrassing church experience. In many cases, stories are likely to originate from visits to churches where kids were unfamiliar with the procedure. If you have kids write out their stories, you have the option of collecting the sheets, reading one story at a time, and letting others guess which story is whose. But there's a lot of material to be covered in this session, so you might want to simply let a few kids relate some anecdotes to help keep the tone of the meeting light and a little more personal.

OPTIONS

SESSION FOUR

MEDIA

SHORT MEETING TIME

URBAN

Step 2
Before the session, record a Christian television broadcast that features a Pentecostal or Charismatic worship service or evangelistic meeting. If possible, try to include segments that feature people speaking in tongues and being "slain in the Spirit." While your group members are watching the tape, ask: **What things do you like about this service? Why? What things make you uncomfortable? Why?** After you get a few responses, move on to Repro Resource 8.

Step 3
To begin this step, play several clips of songs that are sung in different languages. If possible, try to find songs that are sung in Spanish, Italian, German, French, Norwegian, Irish, Japanese, and so forth. See if your group members can identify each foreign language. You might want to make a game out of it by awarding points for each correct answer. Afterward, discuss as a group which of the languages were easiest to identify and which were hardest. Use this activity to introduce the discussion of speaking in tongues.

Step 1
If you're short on time, skip Step 1. To introduce Repro Resource 8 (and the session topic), ask your group members to name the first things that come to mind when you mention the words "Pentecostal" and "Charismatic." Write kids' responses on the board. Then, as you go through Repro Resource 8, compare the information on the sheet with your kids' responses on the board to see how accurate your group members' first impressions were.

Step 4
Rather than going through the statements on Repro Resource 10, ask one of your group members to share an experience he or she had in a Pentecostal/Charismatic church or an encounter he or she had with a Pentecostal/Charismatic acquaintance. Then, as a group, discuss ways that the person might have responded differently (or ways that the person might respond differently in the future). As necessary, incorporate the comments in the session plan concerning the examples on Repro Resource 10.

Step 2
Ask group members to think of the different nationalities that are represented in their neighborhood. Ask: **How many different languages are spoken by the people who live in your area?** See which group member identifies the most languages in his or her neighborhood. Then ask: **How many of these people of other nationalities could you communicate with if you had to?** Get a few responses. Then point out that Peter and the rest of the apostles faced a similar situation at Passover. Lead in to a discussion of Acts 2:1-12. Then hand out copies of Repro Resource 8 and continue the session as written.

Step 4
Invite representatives from one or more Pentecostal or Charismatic churches in your area to your meeting. Ask each representative to talk about some of the things his or her church is doing in the inner city. Perhaps each representative might discuss some of the programs his or her church runs for the homeless and needy, some of the organizations the church sponsors, and so on. After the representatives have shared, spend some time discussing ways that your group could work together with one or more of the churches to further urban ministry in your area.

OPTIONS

SESSION FOUR

Step 3
If your junior highers (or even your high schoolers) aren't familiar with spiritual gifts—what they are or how they are used—take a few minutes to talk about your church's position on spiritual gifts. Read I Corinthians 12:14-31 and Romans 12:3-8. Talk about the different gifts mentioned and how they are visible in your congregation.

Step 4
After reading Galatians 5:22-26, close the session with a fruit party. Bring in nine kinds of fruit, each labeled with a fruit of the spirit. Let the kids put together a fruit salad of their choice. As they're eating, talk about which fruits they see most often and which ones they see least often in people around them. (However, emphasize that no one should mention any names.)

Step 3
One of the best ways to make sure that your group members have a handle on Pentecostal/Charismatic beliefs is to stage a debate. Have kids form two teams. Assign one team to argue from the perspective of Pentecostals and Charismatics. Assign the other team to argue from the perspective of non-Pentecostals and non-Charismatics. Among the topics teams might debate are speaking in tongues, being filled with the Spirit, healing, and being "slain in the Spirit." Give the teams a few minutes to prepare by reviewing Repro Resources, notes from the session, and relevant Scripture passages. In the debate, you will introduce a topic; each team will then have two minutes to present its argument, followed by one minute apiece for each team's rebuttal. Afterward, discuss as a group some of the points that were made during the debate.

Step 4
Bring in several books that explain (in language even a non-seminarian can understand) the beliefs and practices of Pentecostal and Charismatic churches. Give your kids a few minutes to look through the books, marking important sections. Then instruct group members to work together to create a pamphlet that explains how the beliefs and practices of Pentecostals and Charismatics differ from the beliefs and practices of your church. If done well, the pamphlet could be used as a resource in your church's library.

Date Used:

Approx. Time

Step 1: Plan Scan _____
o Extra Action
o Small Group
o Large Group
o Fellowship & Worship
o Extra Fun
o Short Meeting Time
Things needed:

Step 2: How It Started _____
o Extra Action
o Heard It All Before
o Mostly Girls
o Mostly Guys
o Extra Fun
o Media
o Urban
Things needed:

Step 3: Back to the Bible _____
o Small Group
o Large Group
o Little Bible Background
o Media
o Combined Junior High/High School
o Extra Challenge
Things needed:

Step 4: Voices _____
o Heard It All Before
o Little Bible Background
o Fellowship & Worship
o Mostly Girls
o Mostly Guys
o Short Meeting Time
o Urban
o Combined Junior High/High School
o Extra Challenge
Things needed:

SESSION 5

Common Ground and Negotiables

(Affirming the Common Heritage of the Church Universal)

YOUR GOALS FOR THIS SESSION:
Choose one or more

☐ To help kids learn what the Bible teaches about the unity of the church.

☐ To help kids understand which differences between religious groups are important and which are not.

☐ To help kids connect with believers of other denominations.

☐ Other _____

Your Bible Base:

1 Corinthians 1:10-13;
 2:1-5; 3:3-9
Ephesians 4:1-6

CUSTOM CURRICULUM

I've Got Your Number

(Needed: Prepared index cards)

Before the session, you'll need to prepare index cards with the following numbers or number categories on them:
- 28
- Even numbers
- 8
- Any number between 1 and 13
- The last digit of your phone number
- Any number with a 5 or a 3 in it
- Odd numbers
- Your age
- The age of any member of your family
- Numbers that can be divided by 7 with no remainder
- Any number greater than 23

Make sure you have enough cards so that each group member gets one. If you need more cards, come up with numbers or number categories similar to the ones listed above.

To begin the session, hand one card to each group member. Explain: **Each person needs to connect with two other people. You connect by finding a number or number category that you have in common with another person. For example, if your card has "8" on it, you might connect with someone whose card has "Even numbers" on it. When you connect with someone, keep that person by your side. Our goal is to make a circle of connections that includes everyone in the room.**

Give group members a few minutes to search for connections. After a while, you may need to undo some connections in order to regroup in a way that includes everyone. You may also need to "cheat" by claiming a number for yourself that completes the circle.

After you've completed the circle, ask: **How is this circle like the denominations we've been studying?**

If group members can't figure out the connection, say: **Denominations are very different. What can an Anglican possibly share with a Baptist? But what does an even number have in common with an odd number? They're both numbers! And with the help of a few others, we can make a connection.**

If we focus only on our differences, we will always be apart.

But can we find some common ground? Sure we can—in our common worship of Jesus Christ. This is not to say that our differences don't matter. Naturally, we think we have some things right that others have wrong. But we can still talk together, fellowship together, possibly even worship together with those who honor Christ too.

STEP 2

All for One

(Needed: Bibles, copies of Repro Resource 11, pencils)

Have kids form small groups. Hand out copies of "Long Division" (Repro Resource 11) and pencils. Instruct each group to complete all three sections on the sheet. Explain that (a) the author, Paul, had started the church in Corinth a few years earlier; (b) another Christian preacher, Apollos, who was apparently a very skilled preacher, had gained a following in the area; and (c) Cephas was another name for the apostle Peter. (You may want to read Acts 18 yourself as background.)

Give the groups a few minutes to work. When everyone is finished, go through the sheet one section at a time. After each group has shared its title for the first passage, vote as a group on which title is best. Ideally, this voting process will cause some debate among your kids. This activity is designed to stir up division—exactly what the text warns against.

After some debate, ask: **Why does there have to be one supreme title? Can't we learn from the way others have looked at the text?** Get a few responses.

Then say: **In the same way, we can view our faith a certain way, but still learn from people of other denominations.**

Use the following information as needed to supplement your discussion of the Scripture passages on Repro Resource 11.

I Corinthians 1:10-13

What title would you give these verses? (Perhaps "Unity" or "Breaking Up Is Easy to Do.")

What was the problem in Corinth? (Factions. People were arguing over which preacher's teaching to follow.)

Do you think there was anything wrong with the "I follow Christ" group? Explain. (Maybe, maybe not. It's possible that these people were purists who claimed to follow Christ *instead of* other teachers. Or perhaps they thought that they were the only ones who had the truth.)

I Corinthians 2:1-5

How did Paul come to the Corinthians? (He came in weakness and fear, with much trembling. He was not eloquent. In contrast, Apollos was quite eloquent. We know that other preachers of the time prided themselves on their smooth delivery.)

Why was it important for him to come to the Corinthians in this way? Why was it important for him to remind the Corinthians of this? (It was obvious that Paul was not promoting himself when he came to the Corinthians; rather, he was simply preaching God's message.)

What attitude does Paul seem to be recommending for the church? How might that attitude change things? (Perhaps Paul is recommending an attitude of humility and vulnerability. Such an attitude would severely limit the number of arguments and fights in the church.)

I Corinthians 3:3-9

Why does Paul call the Corinthians worldly? (In the world system that doesn't follow Christ, people are always fighting to get their way.)

How does Paul describe Apollos and himself and their work? (Paul described Apollos and himself as "fellow workers," each with a job to do. Their work complemented each other's.)

What do you think is the main point of these verses? (All Christians are teammates in ministry. It's not about us, but about God's work.)

The $64,000,000,000 Question

How do you think Paul's teachings in I Corinthians should affect the way we think about Christian denominations? (Baptists, Presbyterians, Methodists, and the rest may disagree on theological points, but if we are serving Christ, we can work together. We should act with love and humility—and keep the focus on Christ.)

Agreeing to Disagree

(Needed: Copies of Repro Resource 12)

Ask for three volunteers to perform a skit. Hand a copy of "Spies Like Us" (Repro Resource 12) to each volunteer. Give your actors a minute or two to read through the script; then have them perform.

Afterward, ask: **What was the Professor's conclusion?** (The strange beast was an elephant. Each investigator touched only part of it. Since it wasn't a dangerous beast, they could leave it alone.)

Explain: **So it is with denominations sometimes. Each one** focuses on a certain aspect of God, which may be different from the focus of a different denomination.

Is God sovereign, in control of the events of our lives and our world? Absolutely! The Presbyterians have that idea down pat.

Do we also have a responsibility to respond to God's invitations? You bet. That's something the Methodists and Baptists are especially good at.

Can the Holy Spirit be a powerful, transforming force in our lives? Yes! Even if you're not a Pentecostal or Charismatic, you can appreciate their emphasis on the Spirit's power.

The most important thing is Jesus Christ. If we agree that He is our Savior, we can agree to disagree on other issues.

I may like tuna fish and you may hate it. I may think the Dallas Cowboys are the best football team on the planet, and you may violently disagree. I may like classical music and you may despise it. In each case, we can still be friends. We agree to disagree.

In the same way, I may think that the Methodist [or Baptist or Mennonite] church across the street is dead wrong on certain issues. But if we can agree that Jesus Christ died for our sins, we can have fellowship in Christ.

STEP 4

School Days

(Needed: Copies of Repro Resource 13)

Hand out copies of "Alone Together: A Personal Memoir" (Repro Resource 13). Have a volunteer read aloud the "personal memoir."

Afterward, ask: **How does your experience compare with this? How do you normally feel about people of other denominations? How could you establish Christian friendships with people of other denominations?** Get several responses to each of these questions from your group members.

As you wrap up the session, focus on the bottom section of Repro Resource 13, asking group members to consider their response to the series. Give them a minute or two of silence to think and pray about this. Then, to close the session, read aloud Ephesians 4:1-6.

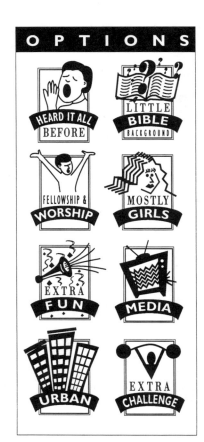

"THEY'RE NOT LIKE US!" REPRO RESOURCE 11

LONG DIVISION

Read each of the passages silently and then discuss the questions that follow.

I Corinthians 1:10-13
What title would you give these verses?

What was the problem in Corinth?

Do you think there was anything wrong with the "I follow Christ" group? Explain.

I Corinthians 2:1-5
How did Paul come to the Corinthians?

Why was it important for him to come to the Corinthians in this way? Why was it important for him to remind the Corinthians of this?

What attitude does Paul seem to be recommending for the church? How might that attitude change things?

I Corinthians 3:3-9
Why does Paul call the Corinthians worldly?

How does Paul describe Apollos and himself and their work?

What do you think is the main point of these verses?

The $64,000,000,000 Question
How do you think Paul's teachings in I Corinthians should affect the way we think about Christian denominations?

"THEY'RE NOT LIKE US!"
SPIES LIKE US

REPRO RESOURCE 12

ALPHONSE: I have called this meeting of our village elders to discuss a serious threat. As you may have heard, there is an invader that comes at night to the lagoon outside the village. Three nights ago, I heard its eerie whining sounds. So, with great courage, I crept out in the darkness to investigate what sort of creature this was.

BERNIE: And what did you find, O Great One?

ALPHONSE: It was dark, you understand, but I managed to touch the beast. It is a thick, tall creature—like a giant tree—with leathery skin.

So I propose that we get the town chainsaw and make this beast into firewood.

BERNIE: I beg to differ, O Great One. Two nights ago, I too crept out to the lagoon under the moonless sky. What I felt with my bare hands was this: a giant worm with two hollow eyes and leathery skin. I propose that we go to the village salt supply and sprinkle salt on this disgusting creature, because we know that salt makes worms shrivel up and die.

CECILIA: I say this with all due respect, but you are both crazy. I went out there last night to check out this thing for myself. It's a bird, I'm telling you. In the darkness, I felt its leathery wing, large and flexible, like the flap of a tent. I fear that this vulture could fly over our town in an instant and devour anyone it set its keen eyes upon. I propose that we take our hairpins and pin its wings down so that it will not be able to fly.

BERNIE: Your idea is really stupid.

CECILIA: *My* idea is stupid? You're going to sprinkle *salt* on the creature! How about a little oregano to go with it?

ALPHONSE: Clearly, you both are missing the point.

CECILIA: I wouldn't talk, Mr. Magoo. Where do you get this "big tree" nonsense anyway?

BERNIE: He probably made a wrong turn and went into the woods. It really *was* a tree!

ALPHONSE: I thought we might have some disagreement, so I invited the Professor and his able assistant, Mary Ann, to hear our testimony and recommend the proper course of action. Professor, you have studied the creatures of many lands. What do you have to say about this strange beast? What is it?

WHAT DID THE PROFESSOR SAY?

"THEY'RE NOT LIKE US!"

REPRO RESOURCE 13

Alone Together:
A Personal Memoir

There was a time when the prophet Elijah thought he was the only true believer in Israel. He thought everyone else had started worshiping idols. "I am the only one left," he cried (I Kings 19:10).

I felt like that as a high school student. But I didn't need to.

I attended an exciting Conservative Baptist church, but most of the kids in my youth group lived in other towns. Only one went to my high school, and she was rather shy. When I looked for Christian fellowship in the halls and classrooms of Gateway High, I couldn't find it.

My classmates were nice, and I got along with them well. Most were Catholic, but some were Methodist and Presbyterian—one even went to a "liberal" Baptist church. But somewhere I got the notion that none of those churches could be trusted. Those kids probably weren't "true" Christians, I thought. They might say they believed in Jesus, but did they really trust Him as their personal Savior? Probably not. I was too bashful to ask them point-blank.

In my senior year, I managed to start a Bible study in a school classroom at the end of the day. (Today I'd get sued for that, but then I wasn't thinking about legal issues.) The Bible study wasn't huge, but maybe a dozen would show up from time to time. And these were Methodists and Presbyterians—people I had written off before. As we talked, I realized these were "true" believers, just as I was, starving for some Christian friendships.

I was sorry it took me that long to reach across those denominational lines. When Elijah was depressed, God reminded him that there were still 7,000 faithful people in Israel. Elijah was not alone. And neither was I.

Based on what we've learned in this series, I think God would like me to . . .
(Check all that apply.)

___ Get to know the beliefs and history of my own denomination.

___ Connect with another Christian in my school or community who may be of another denomination.

___ Explore the beliefs of other denominations.

___ Focus more on the one essential thing: trusting Jesus.

Here's what I can do in the next month to start making that happen:

OPTIONS

SESSION FIVE

Step 1
Begin the session with a game of "Tribond." This board game challenges players to figure out the common bond between three seemingly unrelated items. (For example, if the words "cat," "dog," and "angel" were given, players would have to figure out that they are all types of fish.) Have kids form teams. Rather than having each team move its playing pieces around the game board according to the game's instructions, simply read one set of clues to each team and give the team fifteen seconds to figure out the common bond. Award one point for each correct guess. The team with the most points at the end of the game is the winner. Use this activity to introduce the idea of common bonds between different denominations.

Step 3
Before the session, put together a jigsaw puzzle that has about 100 pieces in it. After putting the puzzle together, divide it into four sections. Put the pieces from each section (after taking them apart) in a separate envelope. At this point in the session, have kids form four teams. Give each team one of the envelopes. Instruct each team to put together its section of the puzzle as quickly as possible. When the teams are finished, put the four sections together to complete the entire puzzle. Use this activity to introduce the idea that different denominations focus on different aspects of God. Suggest that when we look at the emphases of different denominations, we get a better view of the "complete picture" of God.

Step 1
If you don't think you have enough group members to make the number game challenging, try a different activity. Announce that you will do something special for group members (perhaps take them out to eat), if they can list twenty-five different things that they all have in common. This may sound like an unrealistic challenge at first; but after a while, some of your sharper kids will likely begin to expand the perimeters of their thinking. After all, your group members are all people; they're all under ten feet tall; they're all from Earth; and so forth. Keep urging kids on until they find twenty-five reasonably valid things they have in common. Afterward, point out that we tend to treat each other as many church denominations do—we tend to focus much more on our differences than we do on our similarities.

Step 2
Conduct the Bible study as a single group, letting different people read the Scripture passages and respond to the questions (though after the first person answers, try to encourage additional comments or differences of opinion from others). It shouldn't take long for a small group to get through these questions and have a reasonably in-depth discussion. At the end of the study, add a few questions: **What do you think our church needs to learn from Paul's writings? What is the most important thing you think *you* should remember from these passages? Have you ever been involved in "competition" of a spiritual nature? If so, what was the situation? How was it resolved?**

Step 1
The numbers activity may be difficult for a large group, so you may want to replace it with a different opener. Divide your kids into groups of six, trying as much as possible to separate kids who usually hang around together. Hand out paper and pencils to each group. Explain that the groups will be competing to see which one can form the strongest bond among its members. The members of each group will form their bonds by finding things that *all* of them have in common. The team that comes up with the longest list of common bonds in five minutes is the winner. Encourage kids to be as imaginative as possible in their lists. Emphasize that almost nothing is too obscure to be considered a common bond. (For example, if all six group members were born in an even-numbered month, that would be considered an acceptable common bond.) After five minutes, collect the lists and read each one aloud. Award prizes to the group with the longest list. Use this activity to introduce the topic of common bonds between different denominations.

Step 3
After volunteers go through the skit on Repro Resource 12, have group members form teams. Instruct each team to create a riddle scenario similar to the one on Repro Resource 12, in which three different characters have three different (limited) views as to what something is. After a few minutes, have each team share its riddle scenario. See if any of your other group members can solve the riddle. Afterward, draw comparisons to the way different denominations focus on different aspects of God.

OPTIONS

SESSION FIVE

HEARD IT ALL BEFORE

Step 3
Kids who have spent most of their lives in the same church may assume that all church worship services are fairly standard. If such is the case with your group members, try an activity that will help your kids recognize the differences (as well as some of the similarities) between the worship services of various denominations. During the week before the session, collect several bulletins (or sheets that list the order of service) from several different churches (of different denominations) in your area. Let your group members look through the bulletins, noting similarities and differences of worship procedures in the various churches. Is the order of service relatively consistent from church to church? Do any of the churches include worship elements that your church doesn't? Are any of the same hymns sung in different churches? Do the sermon topics have anything in common? After a few minutes, discuss your group members' findings.

Step 4
As you wrap up the session (and this series), throw a curveball at your heard-it-all-before kids. After discussing the common ground of different denominations, ask: **If Christians have these things in common, then why do we need denominations?** Group members' answers to this question should give you a clue as to how well they've been listening during the past few weeks. As needed, review material from the first four sessions of the book.

LITTLE BIBLE BACKGROUND

Step 2
The Bible passages covered are good ones for a group without much Bible background. But you might want to take an approach other than simply asking the questions presented in the session. Instead, ask your group members to suppose that they are writing a book entitled *Everything You Need to Know about Starting a Church and Keeping It Going Strong*. Explain that these passages have been recommended as excellent sources for research. After you read each passage, ask: **What can we learn about starting and maintaining a church from this source? What would be a good chapter title to describe this information? Can you think of personal stories from our church or youth group that might be included in this chapter?**

Step 4
This series covers a lot of material that your group members are likely to forget before long. So try to give kids something to remember. As time permits at the end of the session, see how much of the closing passage (Ephesians 4:1-6) kids can memorize before they leave. Start by having kids first memorize verses 4-6. Then, if there is still time, go back to verse 3; then to verse 2; and, last but not least, to verse 1. Some of your better memorizers may be able to quote the entire passage by the time they leave. If so, challenge them to keep saying it every day for a while until they are sure they won't forget it.

FELLOWSHIP & WORSHIP

Step 1
To begin the session, say: **So far in this series, we've learned a lot about different denominations. Let's list some of the things that we've learned.** Encourage group members to name some similarities and differences between your church's denomination and other denominations. Also encourage kids to share things they've learned about other denominations that they didn't know before. Afterward, read Ephesians 4:1-6. Talk about the fact that ultimately, we all focus on God. Spend a few minutes in prayer, thanking God for creating both unity and diversity.

Step 4
The best way for your kids to understand another denomination is to visit a worship service. Line up some visits for your youth group to various area churches. You may even wish to talk to other youth leaders to set up a time of sharing between the two groups. Continually remind your group members that regardless of our differences, all denominations have the same goal—to worship and honor God.

OPTIONS

SESSION FIVE

Mostly Girls

Step 1
Have your girls form groups of three or four. Ask the members of each group to describe what they think the church universal might be like if we humans didn't get so caught up in focusing on everyone's differences. Let group members use paper, pencils, crayons, markers, magazines, or anything else they need to create a representation of their "united" church. They may use words, pictures, colors, or anything they want. After a few minutes, ask each group to share and explain its creation.

Step 4
After your girls have completed Repro Resource 13, encourage them to share with the group some of their thoughts on this series—what they've learned and what they need to work on. Then have group members form pairs. Instruct the members of each pair to pray for each other, mentioning specifically the goals for the next month as listed on Repro Resource 13. Close the session by reading Ephesians 4:1-6 and offering prayer for the group as whole.

Mostly Guys

Step 1
Tailor the categories of the number game specifically to guys and then let them play it as written. Here are some categories to get you started:
• Number of times you've worn your gym shorts since you washed them
• Number of times you've eaten today
• Number of girls you've had a crush on this year
• The last two numbers of anyone's phone number you know from memory
• Number of CDs you've bought during the past month
• Number on any uniform you've ever worn

Step 3
Try to convey the information in this step in the form of a couple of skits. Have two volunteers play the roles of guys who are meeting for the first time. The first guy should try to start a conversation to get to know the other guy better. But the second guy should strongly disagree with every opinion the first guy expresses. Group members should see clearly how difficult it is to make new friends while maintaining a negative attitude. Then do a second skit in which the first guy does exactly the same thing—tries to get to know the other guy. But this time, the second guy—while he may disagree with the first guy's opinions—should try to do so in a gentle way that would not offend him. In many cases, he might agree up to a point, but then express a slight difference of opinion. Your guys should see that the attitudes they have toward other people may be much more important than they realize. Ask: **What can we learn from these two skits about getting along with people who belong to other denominations?**

Extra Fun

Step 1
Have kids form two teams to play "tug-of-war." Start by using a cheap piece of thin string or ribbon that is sure to break. Try again by doubling the string, then tripling it, and so forth, until it eventually becomes unbreakable. Afterward, point out that our "ties" to other people may be broken if we have only one thing in common with them. But the better we become at finding additional ties and common bonds, the stronger the connection becomes. Soon the relationship becomes so strong that, no matter how hard we pull (or how much we disagree), the bond will not break. We need to develop as many common bonds as we can with people of other denominations before we start focusing on differences of opinions.

Step 4
Conclude the session by having your kids play a few rounds of the game Taboo. The object of the game is to communicate a word or phrase to someone else without using five "taboo" words. After playing a while, point out that with practice, we can learn to communicate with people of other denominations without keying on the things that cause disagreement. Emphasize that we need to practice focusing on the things that are OK to discuss before we move on to more "taboo" areas of conversation.

OPTIONS

SESSION FIVE

Step 1
Play portions of three seemingly unrelated songs and see if your kids can guess what the common bond is that links the three songs. For example, you might play "Hey Jude" by the Beatles, "The End of the Road" by Boyz II Men, and "She Talks to Angels" by the Black Crowes. The common bond is that the songs are all performed by groups whose names start with the letter "B." Play three or four rounds, using a different set of songs for each round. Depending on how well-versed your group members are in pop music, you may make the common bonds as obvious or as obscure as you like. Use this activity to introduce the idea of common bonds between different denominations.

Step 4
Bring in a couple of videos that contain scenes of people coming together for a common purpose. For example, you might show the scene at the end of *It's a Wonderful Life* in which all of George Bailey's friends gather to help him out. Or you might show the scene at the end of *How the Grinch Stole Christmas* in which the residents of Whoville join together to celebrate Christmas. After showing the scenes, ask: **Is this how you picture people of different denominations coming together? If not, how do you picture it?** Use the ensuing discussion to get ideas from your group members on how they might go about establishing contact with kids from other denominations.

Step 1
Rather than using the numbers activity, try a shorter opener. Have kids form groups of three or four. Give each group a piece of paper and a pencil. See which group can be the first to discover ten things that all of its members have in common. The first team to list ten common bonds and then hand its list to you is the winner. Use this activity to introduce the topic of common bonds between different denominations.

Step 2
If you're short on time, use only the I Corinthians 1:10-13 and I Corinthians 3:3-9 passages on Repro Resource 11. Rather than having kids form small groups to assign titles to the passages, simply read each passage and then discuss as a group the questions on the sheet. In Step 3, skip Repro Resource 12. Briefly point out the emphases of different denominations and affirm that the important thing is that we agree that Jesus is our Savior. Then move on to Step 4 to wrap up the session (and the series).

Step 3
Before you begin Step 4, ask your group members to list some of the obstacles that prevent or hinder them from getting to know people of other denominations. Encourage kids to call out as many obstacles as they can think of, no matter how minor the obstacles may seem. Compile a list on the board of the obstacles your group members name. After you've got a fairly sizable list, brainstorm as a group some ways to overcome the obstacles listed on the board. Your group members may surprise you (and themselves) with the helpful suggestions they come up with. Encourage each person to choose one of the suggestions to put to use this week to establish contact with someone from another denomination. Allow some time at the beginning of your next meeting for group members to share the results of their efforts.

Step 4
As you wrap up this session (and this series), have your kids plan a community project that will include youth groups from several different churches (of different denominations) in your area. Perhaps you might plan a cleanup day at a local park or playground in which young people can work side by side with members of other churches to beautify the community. Or perhaps you might contact a local mission or homeless shelter to see what your group of interdenominational kids can do there. Your goal is to help kids see what they can accomplish when they work in cooperation with fellow believers.

OPTIONS

S E S S I O N   F I V E

Step 1
Ask your junior highers to move to one side of the room and your high schoolers to move to the other side. Explain that you will be calling out "dividers," things that will cause your kids to choose one side of an issue or another. To indicate their responses, kids will move to one side of the room or the other. For instance, you might say: **I believe that capital punishment is OK.** If kids agree with the statement, they should move to one side of the room; if they disagree, they should move to the other side. Spend a few minutes calling out a variety of dividers—some significant, some not. At various points throughout the game, point out that each side of the room contains both junior highers and high schoolers. At the end of the game, when kids are thoroughly combined, say: **Though we all didn't agree on all of the same things, it's clear that some of us have things in common that we didn't realize before.** Point out that the same is true with the church. Some denominations have more in common with certain denominations than with others, but we all have a common ground—Jesus Christ.

Step 2
If you know that your junior highers will have trouble with Repro Resource 11, you may wish to try another option. Before the session, prepare a poster that summarizes the main points of each passage on Repro Resource 11. At this point in the session, read each portion of Scripture, talk about the main points you've summarized, and then ask volunteers to act out how they think the Corinthians might have reacted to Paul's message or how Paul might have delivered it. Encourage group members to look at each passage from various angles to see what they come up with.

Step 3
At the end of Step 3, before you wrap up the session (and the series), give your kids a chance to test each other on what they've learned during the past few weeks. Have kids form two teams. Instruct each team to come up with seven questions that deal with denominations. The questions may address historical information about denominations (who started which denomination and why), scriptural principles, specific beliefs of various denominations, or any other denomination-related topic. However, the teams *must* know the correct answer for each question they come up with. After a few minutes, let the teams take turns firing questions at one another. Award one point for each time a team correctly answers one of its opponent's questions and one point for each time a team stumps its opponent with a question. If you wish, give prizes to the team with the most points at the end of the game.

Step 4
Instruct your group members to do some research to find out what constitutes the "common ground" that most denominations and Christian groups agree on. If your kids are really ambitious, you might have them schedule times to talk with the pastors or board members of other churches (of different denominations) in your area to find out specific information regarding each church's beliefs and practices. Your kids can use the information they compile to plan an interdenominational worship service with several of the churches in your area.

Date Used: Approx.
                                         Time

Step 1: I've Got Your Number   _____
o Extra Action
o Small Group
o Large Group
o Fellowship & Worship
o Mostly Girls
o Mostly Guys
o Extra Fun
o Media
o Short Meeting Time
o Combined Junior High/High School
Things needed:

Step 2: All for One   _____
o Small Group
o Little Bible Background
o Short Meeting Time
o Combined Junior High/High School
Things needed:

Step 3: Agreeing to Disagree   _____
o Extra Action
o Large Group
o Heard It All Before
o Mostly Guys
o Urban
o Extra Challenge
Things needed:

Step 4: School Days   _____
o Heard It All Before
o Little Bible Background
o Fellowship & Worship
o Mostly Girls
o Extra Fun
o Media
o Urban
o Extra Challenge
Things needed:

93

Custom Curriculum Critique

Please take a moment to fill out this evaluation form, rip it out, fold it, tape it, and send it back to us. This will help us continue to customize products for you. Thanks!

1. Overall, please give this *Custom Curriculum* course (*"They're Not Like Us!"*) a grade in terms of how well it worked for you. (A=excellent; B=above average; C=average; D=below average; F=failure) Circle one.

    A   B   C   D   F

2. Now assign a grade to each part of this curriculum that you used.

a. Upfront article	A	B	C	D	F	Didn't use
b. Publicity/Clip art	A	B	C	D	F	Didn't use
c. Repro Resource Sheets	A	B	C	D	F	Didn't use
d. Session 1	A	B	C	D	F	Didn't use
e. Session 2	A	B	C	D	F	Didn't use
f. Session 3	A	B	C	D	F	Didn't use
g. Session 4	A	B	C	D	F	Didn't use
h. Session 5	A	B	C	D	F	Didn't use

3. How helpful were the options?
    - ❏ Very helpful
    - ❏ Somewhat helpful
    - ❏ Not too helpful
    - ❏ Not at all helpful

4. Rate the amount of options:
    - ❏ Too many
    - ❏ About the right amount
    - ❏ Too few

5. Tell us how often you used each type of option (4=Always; 3=Sometimes; 2=Seldom; 1=Never)

	4	3	2	1
Extra Action	❏	❏	❏	❏
Combined Jr. High/High School	❏	❏	❏	❏
Urban	❏	❏	❏	❏
Small Group	❏	❏	❏	❏
Large Group	❏	❏	❏	❏
Extra Fun	❏	❏	❏	❏
Heard It All Before	❏	❏	❏	❏
Little Bible Background	❏	❏	❏	❏
Short Meeting Time	❏	❏	❏	❏
Fellowship and Worship	❏	❏	❏	❏
Mostly Guys	❏	❏	❏	❏
Mostly Girls	❏	❏	❏	❏
Media	❏	❏	❏	❏
Extra Challenge (High School only)	❏	❏	❏	❏
Sixth Grade (Jr. High only)	❏	❏	❏	❏

(tape here)

BUSINESS REPLY MAIL
FIRST CLASS MAIL   PERMIT NO 1   ELGIN IL

POSTAGE WILL BE PAID BY ADDRESSEE
Attn: Youth Department

David C Cook Publishing Co
850 N GROVE AVE
ELGIN IL 60120-9980

NO POSTAGE
NECESSARY
IF MAILED
IN THE
UNITED STATES

---

6. What did you like best about this course?

7. What suggestions do you have for improving *Custom Curriculum*?

8. Other topics you'd like to see covered in this series:

9. Are you?
   ❏ Full time paid youthworker
   ❏ Part time paid youthworker
   ❏ Volunteer youthworker

10. When did you use *Custom Curriculum*?
    ❏ Sunday School   ❏ Small Group
    ❏ Youth Group   ❏ Retreat
    ❏ Other _____

---

11. What grades did you use it with? _____

12. How many kids used the curriculum in an average week? _____

13. What's the approximate attendance of your entire Sunday school program (Nursery through Adult)? _____

14. If you would like information on other *Custom Curriculum* courses, or other youth products from David C. Cook, please fill out the following:

    Name: _____
    Church Name: _____
    Address: _____

    Phone: (____) _____

Thank you!